Current
CONTROVERSIES

Global Warming

Other Books in the Current Controversies Series

Global Warming

Debra A. Miller, Book Editor

GREENHAVEN PRESS
A part of Gale, Cengage Learning

GALE
CENGAGE Learning·

Detroit • New York • San Francisco • New Haven, Conn • Waterville, Maine • London

Christine Nasso, *Publisher*
Elizabeth Des Chenes, *Managing Editor*

© 2008 Greenhaven Press, a part of Gale, Cengage Learning

Gale and Greenhaven Press are registered trademarks used herein under license.

For more information, contact:
Greenhaven Press
27500 Drake Rd.
Farmington Hills, MI 48331-3535
Or you can visit our Internet site at gale.cengage.com

Articles in Greenhaven Press anthologies are often edited for length to meet page require-ments. In addition, original titles of these works are changed to clearly present the main thesis and to explicitly indicate the author's opinion. Every effort is made to ensure that Greenhaven Press accurately reflects the original intent of the authors. Every effort has been made to trace the owners of copyrighted material.

Cover image copyright Armin Ropse, 2008. Used under license from Shutterstock.com.

LIBRARY OF CONGRESS CATALOGING-IN-PUBLICATION DATA

Global warming / Debra A. Miller, book editor.
  p. cm. -- (Current controversies)
Includes bibliographical references and index.
ISBN-13: 978-0-7377-4070-7 (hardcover)
ISBN-13: 978-0-7377-4071-4 (pbk.)
1. Global warming. I. Miller, Debra A.
  QC981.8.G56G574414 2008
  363.738'74--dc22

                                                          2008001004

Printed in the United States of America
1 2 3 4 5   12 11 10 09 08

ED102

Contents

Chapter 1: Is Global Warming a Real Problem?

Jeff Severns Guntzel

It is indisputable that humans are releasing carbon dioxide into the atmosphere, adding to the "greenhouse effect," but for decades there has been a debate in the scientific community about what the consequences will be for the planet.

Yes: Global Warming Is a Real Problem

Sandi Doughton

Although most scientists originally did not believe in global warming, every major scientific body to examine the evidence in recent years has concluded that the planet is getting hotter due to human activities, and that it is to get worse.

Environment News Service

The United Nations' Intergovernmental Panel on Climate Change, IPCC, in a 2007 report, concluded that changes in the Earth's atmosphere, oceans, glaciers, and ice caps show unequivocally that the Earth is warming as a result of human activities.

In a 2007 report released by the United Nations Inter-governmental Panel on Climate Change (IPCC), leading climate scientists from 113 countries say that human activities, such as use of fossil fuels like oil and gas and agricultural practices, are the principle cause of rising temperatures.

Chapter 3: What Are the Potential Threats from Global Warming?

As the Earth's temperatures rise, scientists expect to see changes in infectious disease patterns, such as an increase in cases of malaria, year-round influenza, and an increased transmission of a variety of other diseases.

Chapter 4: What Action Should Be Taken to Reduce Global Warming?

Foreword

By definition, controversies are "discussions of questions in which opposing opinions clash" (Webster's Twentieth Century Dictionary Unabridged). Few would deny that controversies are a pervasive part of the human condition and exist on virtually every level of human enterprise. Controversies transpire between individuals and among groups, within nations and between nations. Controversies supply the grist necessary for progress by providing challenges and challengers to the status quo. They also create atmospheres where strife and warfare can flourish. A world without controversies would be a peaceful world; but it also would be, by and large, static and prosaic.

The Series' Purpose

The purpose of the Current Controversies series is to explore many of the social, political, and economic controversies dominating the national and international scenes today. Titles selected for inclusion in the series are highly focused and specific. For example, from the larger category of criminal justice, Current Controversies deals with specific topics such as police brutality, gun control, white collar crime, and others. The debates in Current Controversies also are presented in a useful, timeless fashion. Articles and book excerpts included in each title are selected if they contribute valuable, long-range ideas to the overall debate. And wherever possible, current information is enhanced with historical documents and other relevant materials. Thus, while individual titles are current in focus, every effort is made to ensure that they will not become quickly outdated. Books in the Current Controversies series will remain important resources for librarians, teachers, and students for many years.

In addition to keeping the titles focused and specific, great care is taken in the editorial format of each book in the series. Book introductions and chapter prefaces are offered to provide background material for readers. Chapters are organized around several key questions that are answered with diverse opinions representing all points on the political spectrum. Materials in each chapter include opinions in which authors clearly disagree as well as alternative opinions in which authors may agree on a broader issue but disagree on the possible solutions. In this way, the content of each volume in Current Controversies mirrors the mosaic of opinions encountered in society. Readers will quickly realize that there are many viable answers to these complex issues. By questioning each author's conclusions, students and casual readers can begin to develop the critical thinking skills so important to evaluating opinionated material.

Current Controversies is also ideal for controlled research. Each anthology in the series is composed of primary sources taken from a wide gamut of informational categories including periodicals, newspapers, books, U.S. and foreign government documents, and the publications of private and public organizations. Readers will find factual support for reports, debates, and research papers covering all areas of important issues. In addition, an annotated table of contents, an index, a book and periodical bibliography, and a list of organizations to contact are included in each book to expedite further research.

Perhaps more than ever before in history, people are confronted with diverse and contradictory information. During the Persian Gulf War, for example, the public was not only treated to minute-to-minute coverage of the war, it was also inundated with critiques of the coverage and countless analyses of the factors motivating U.S. involvement. Being able to sort through the plethora of opinions accompanying today's major issues, and to draw one's own conclusions, can be a complicated and frustrating struggle. It is the editors' hope that Current Controversies will help readers with this struggle.

Introduction

"Although all of the methods of global warming study have some scientific uncertainties, each has reached the same conclusion—that the Earth has warmed dramatically over the last 100 years."

Scientists have known since the discovery of the early ice ages in the eighteenth century that the Earth's climate can change dramatically due to natural causes, but the dawn of the industrial age—and the burning of fossil fuels such as coal and oil—caused speculation about whether human activities might also affect the climate. In 1896, for example, Swedish scientist Svante Arrhenius became the first to suggest that the burning of these fossil fuels, by adding carbon dioxide gas to the Earth's atmosphere, could raise the planet's average temperature. At the time, Arrhenius's discovery of this "greenhouse effect" was quickly dismissed by the mainstream scientific community, which reasoned that such a major climate change would not likely be produced by mere humans and could only happen slowly over tens of thousands of years.

By the 1950s, however, scientists' understanding of climate changes had improved dramatically, largely because of sharp increases in funding due to the military's rising interest in weather forecasting. Studies at this time showed that the atmospheric carbon dioxide buildup could produce rising temperatures. In 1961, studies confirmed that carbon dioxide levels were indeed rising year after year. Modern instruments also showed clearly that the Earth is warming—specifically that the mean annual surface air temperatures of the Earth had risen approximately 0.5°C (0.9°F) since 1860.

Over the next several decades, scientists used a variety of methods to study exactly how the Earth's temperature is changing. Some scientists studied ancient tree rings, corals, fossils, pollens, sediment cores, ice cores, and cave stalactites—called paleoclimatic data—to compare ancient temperatures with modern data. This paleoclimatic record allowed researchers to examine global temperature fluctuations over the last several centuries and even further back in time. Still other researchers devised mathematical models of the climate, which allowed for predictions to be made about temperature changes when the amount of carbon dioxide input was increased. In the late twentieth century, these models were greatly improved by the use of computers, which can incorporate massive amounts of weather information into the climate formulas and produce much more accurate predictions of future climate changes. Also between 1985 and the early 2000s, scientists began to use satellites to observe the Earth's changing climate. Although all of the methods of global warming study have some scientific uncertainties, each has reached the same conclusion—that the Earth has warmed dramatically over the last 100 years.

The scientific consensus about climate change, however, is a fairly recent phenomenon. As recently as the 1960s and 1970s, scientists believed that average temperatures might rise just a few degrees in the next century—not a change that seemed to require immediate policy revision. In addition, some scientists were equally concerned about the effects of smog, which could potentially block sunlight and cause the world to cool, rather than heat up. Indeed, a cooling trend was recorded between the 1940s and 1970s, when air pollution became a serious problem in various countries including the United States. Most scientists at this time agreed only that the Earth's climate was very complicated and that much more research was needed before accurate predictions about the effect of human activity on climate change could be made.

As a result, decades of additional research followed, including the collection of massive amounts of weather data by ocean-going ships and Earth-orbiting satellites and consultation among scientists around the globe. As information about the climate increased, a growing number of scientists became more convinced of the existence and potentially serious impacts of global warming. Many climate researchers began to warn policy makers and the public of the need to address the problem. The issue of global warming received widespread publicity first in the summer of 1988, when temperatures soared to the highest levels on record.

Finally, an independent panel of scientists was assembled by the world's governments to look into the matter. Created by the United Nations in 1988, the Intergovernmental Panel on Climate Change (IPCC) was charged with examining the available scientific, technical, and socioeconomic evidence on the risk of human-induced climate change and providing advice to the international community about the impact and possible solutions. During its early years, the IPCC supported a UN treaty on global warming, called the UN Framework Convention on Climate Change (UNFCCC), adopted in 1992, and helped to provide information for negotiations that led to the 1997 adoption of the Kyoto Protocol—an international agreement that set binding targets for the reduction of greenhouse emissions by developed countries.

In 2001, the IPCC announced a consensus of the world's scientists: The Earth is facing a major problem of global warming due to greenhouse gas emissions released by the burning of fossil fuels. This widely reported assessment helped to convince many people that climate change is a serious environmental, social, and political problem. Yet the report conceded that there were still some scientific uncertainties about the causes and impacts of global warming that required additional study.

Six years later, in February 2007, the IPCC released its Fourth Assessment Report that made an even stronger case for the dangers of global warming. This report concluded that global warming is "unequivocal," and that the world's rising temperatures are "very likely" (defined as 90 percent certainty) to be the result of human activities such as the burning of fossil fuels. The report confirmed that current atmospheric levels of carbon dioxide and methane, two important greenhouse gases, have increased at an unprecedented rate since the late-eighteenth-century onset of the industrial revolution.

The results of this significant increase in greenhouse emissions, the report found, are rising temperatures, severe weather, rising sea levels, and melting glacier ice. The report asserted that the future impact of global warming depended on the level of future greenhouse emissions. Even the best case scenarios, however, were anticipated to bring more warming and continued climate changes. But if humans took no action to limit global warming, the report warned, there would be twice as much warming, with even more dire climatic impacts.

Many commentators concluded that the 2007 IPCC report removed all uncertainties about global warming, showing that climate change is one of mankind's most urgent problems. Despite this convergence of opinion on the dangers of global warming, however, skeptics remained, some of them scientists who continued to conduct research attempting to disprove mainstream scientific conclusions on this issue. The authors in *Current Controversies: Global Warming* present a full range of perspectives on various aspects of the climate change phenomenon.

CHAPTER 1

Is Global Warming a Real Problem?

Chapter Overview

Jeff Severns Guntzel

Jeff Severns Guntzel is a staff writer for the National Catholic Reporter.

The debate over global warming is experiencing a sort of freeze. Gallup Polls taken [in 2001 and 2005] show no . . . change in the percentage of Americans polled who believe the effects of global warming have already begun to happen: 54 percent. It's a dubious indicator, however, in the face of polls that betray a widespread ignorance of even the most fundamental principles of global warming theory among Americans. Part of this, no doubt, is the nature of the popular discussion over climate change. "Much of the debate on global climate change seems polarized and partisan," the . . . [U.S. Conference of Catholic Bishops] wrote in 2001. "Science is too often used as a weapon, not as a source of wisdom. Various interests use the airwaves and political process to minimize or exaggerate the challenges we face."

These things are indisputable: There is something called the "greenhouse effect." It's simple, really. Naturally occurring "greenhouse gases" in the atmosphere—including carbon dioxide—trap some of the sun's heat on the earth, keeping the planet warm. The greenhouse effect is good—until it is bad. Human industry is adding carbon dioxide to the atmosphere. Most notably, it's coming from our cars and our coal-burning power plants. When scientists, environmentalists or politicians talk about global warming, they are talking about human interference with what is otherwise a natural phenomenon: the greenhouse effect.

And this is where the disputable—or at least the disputed—part comes in. That humans are releasing additional greenhouse gases into the atmosphere is not in dispute. The consequences for the future of the planet, however, are contested—sometimes hotly. Mostly, the debate inside the scientific community is about how serious the consequences will be.

Layers of Scientific Specialties

When Spencer Weart, a science historian and author of *The Discovery of Global Warming*, gives presentations on the subject, he begins with a slide of a diagram connecting the infinite layers of scientific specialties concerned with some aspect of climate change and its consequences. There is paleontology, solar physics, space physics, volcanology, palynology (the study of ancient pollens), ice dynamics, computer science, celestial mechanics . . . the list is interminable and, to the layperson, often unintelligible. At some point in his specialists' roll call— likely somewhere around the study of ancient pollens part— people start to laugh. Weart's message is obvious: It's a complicated matter.

One obstacle to an uncomplicated discussion of global warming is the degree of uncertainty inherent to any scientific process.

Or it's quite simple. British journalist George Monbiot has been covering the political and scientific debate over global warming for more than a decade. In a recent article, written earlier this year [2005] on the eve of the hard-won and tenuous launch of the U.N. Kyoto Protocol [an international treaty] in which industrialized nations agreed to reduce greenhouse gases, Monbiot began in his garden: "It is now mid-February," he wrote, "and already I have sown 11 species of vegetable. I know, though the seed packets tell me otherwise, that they will flourish. Everything in this country—daffodils, primroses, almond trees, bumblebees, nesting birds—is a month ahead of schedule. And it feels wonderful. Winter is no longer the great grey longing of my childhood."

A Pentagon report released in late 2003 titled, "An Abrupt Climate Change Scenario and Its Implications for United States National Security," looked to a different backyard: "We have created a climate change scenario," the report's authors began, "that although not the most likely, is plausible, and would challenge United States national security in ways that should be considered immediately." "As famine, disease and weather-related disasters strike due to the abrupt climate change," the report speculated, "many countries' needs will exceed their carrying capacity. This will create a sense of desperation, which is likely to lead to offensive aggression in order to reclaim balance. Imagine eastern European countries, struggling to feed their populations with a falling supply of food, water and energy, eyeing Russia, whose population is already in decline, for access to its grain, minerals and energy supply. Or, picture Japan, suffering from flooding along its coastal cities and contamination of its fresh water supply, eyeing Russia's Sakhalin Island oil and gas reserves as an energy source to power desalination plants and energy-intensive agricultural processes. Envision Pakistan, India and China—all armed with nuclear weapons—skirmishing at their borders over refugees, access to shared rivers, and arable land. Spanish and Portuguese fishermen might fight over fishing rights—leading to conflicts at sea . . ." Surely you get the idea.

A Degree of Uncertainty

One obstacle to an uncomplicated discussion of global warming is the degree of uncertainty inherent to any scientific process. The processes used to measure the extent of human interference with the Earth's atmosphere and the potential consequences are no exception.

The degree of uncertainty was high in 1979 when, at the urging of President Jimmy Carter, a nine-member panel, known officially as the "Ad Hoc Study Group on Carbon Dioxide and Climate," and unofficially as the "Charney panel," undertook one of the first major scientific inquiries into the potential consequences of human interference with the Earth's atmosphere. "If carbon dioxide continues to increase," the Charney panel concluded, there is "no reason to doubt that climate changes will result and no reason to believe that these changes will be negligible." "We may not be given warning" the panel said, before the level of carbon dioxide in the atmosphere is so great that "climate change is inevitable."

Spencer Weart calls the Charney panel "remarkably prescient." "In 1979," said Weart, "they said this is a serious issue and there's going to be a 20-year time lag before it starts to show up—they had it nailed already back then and they were fairly limited, they were all basically computer meteorologists."

Climate change is for real.

After the Charney panel, independent international scientists from a wider range of specialties began to meet about climate change. The [Ronald] Reagan administration came in on the heels of the Charney panel's report and, according to Weart, "began to get disturbed" as more international attention was given to the issue of climate change and its ramifications. Disturbed by attention to the findings, not by the findings themselves, the administration began pushing for an intergovernmental panel. "Something where all the scientists are appointed by governments," Weart said, "and where all the science has to be vetted by government representatives."

That intergovernmental panel came into being in 1988. The International Panel on Climate Change [IPCC] was a joint creation of the World Meteorological Organization and the U.N. Environment Program and was open to all members of the United Nations. "It's not generally recognized," said Weart, "that the IPCC was a conservative response to the fear that the environmentalists—who tended to be identified with scientists—would run away with [the issue]."

Today, it is likely that [the] [George W.] Bush administration feels that the international panel itself—which has become the preeminent source for information on global climate change—has "run away" with the conversation. In 2002, when the term of the international panel's outspoken chairman Robert Watson was to expire, the Bush administration, following a lobbying effort by the energy industry, chose not to renominate the respected atmospheric chemist for the post he had held since 1996. Instead, the administration, characterized by its ambiguous rejection of much of the panel's assertions, nominated Indian engineer and economist Dr. Rajendra K. Pachauri, who won the seat and still serves today.

Labeled the "let's drag our feet" candidate by former Vice President Al Gore, Pachauri surprised all sides recently when, in January [2005], he told representatives of 114 governments attending an international conference in Mauritius [an island country off the east coast of Africa], "Climate change is for real." Calling for serious cuts in pollution, Pachauri declared, "We have just a small window of opportunity and it is closing rather rapidly. There is not a moment to lose." Speaking with the confidence of nearly two decades of research by the International Panel on Climate Change, Pachauri declared, "We are risking the ability of the human race to survive."

Critics of global warming . . . often seize on the necessary uncertainty of scientific process.

That the head of a body that includes 2,500 scientists—all working in some capacity to understand climate change and its consequences—would make such an unambiguous statement about global warming was made doubly significant by

George W. Bush's State of the Union address just weeks later: The president did not once utter the words "global warming" or "climate change."

In his first presidential address on global warming, Bush acknowledged much of what proponents of global warming had been saying for years. But he also highlighted the uncertainties. "We do not know how much effect natural fluctuations in climate may have had on warming," Bush said on the White House lawn. "We do not know how much our climate could, or will change in the future. We do not know how fast change will occur, or even how some of our actions could impact it."

"The scientific community," Weart said, "has not much narrowed the range of uncertainty since the Charney committee. In fact, if anything, the range of uncertainty has broadened as we become aware of the way that atmospheric pressure has been masking the effect of global warming so that the most important degree of uncertainty right now is what the most important biological component of the world will do, which means us." Critics of global warming science, it seems, often seize on the necessary uncertainty of scientific process.

Hockey Stick Graph

Much of the most recent wave of challenges to the theory of global warming centers on something called the "Hockey Stick," a graph depicting an essentially flat global temperature throughout much of the previous one thousand years and a sharp spike—like the end of a hockey stick—beginning in the 1900s.

Adopted and popularized by the International Panel on Climate Change in 2001, the graph has been a point of contention ever since. Critics say the flat graph does not account for events with names like the "Medieval Warming Period" and the "Little Ice Age." But Michael Mann, the climatologist most responsible for the graph, points out that these are re-gional phenomena and that the hockey stick measures global temperature.

The most prominent forces criticizing global warming theory have direct ties ... to the energy industry.

And, though he has conceded to some minor criticisms, Mann points out that his "hockey stick" is not, as the attacks tend to purport, the centerpiece of global warming theory—even if it is one of its most famous illustrations. There exists, Mann says, an entire "hockey team" of evidence that predates his graph and much evidence presented since. "There's this huge body of data," said Weart, "and then somebody will pick one piece of it and they'll find some flaw in it—or else they'll come up with some new piece of data and say, 'See, this in-validates everything.' And then there is a brouhaha over this one very narrow aspect of the question."

Further complicating things is the question of funding. The most prominent forces criticizing global warming theory have direct ties—sometimes to the tune of hundreds of thou-sands of dollars—to the energy industry, which has significant interest in staving off any movement towards strict regulation and costly obedience. So the conversation stalls. Whom do you trust?

Scientists Have Reached a Consensus About Global Warming

Sandi Doughton

Sandi Doughton is a staff reporter for the Seattle Times, *a U.S. newspaper.*

1995 was the hottest year on record until it was eclipsed by 1997—then 1998, 2001, 2002, 2003 and 2004. Melting ice has driven Alaska Natives from seal-hunting areas used for generations. Glaciers around the globe are shrinking so rapidly many could disappear before the middle of the century. As one study after another has pointed to carbon dioxide and other man-made emissions as the most plausible explanation, the cautious community of science has embraced an idea initially dismissed as far-fetched. The result is a convergence of opinion rarely seen in a profession where attacking each other's work is part of the process. Every major scientific body to examine the evidence has come to the same conclusion: The planet is getting hotter; man is to blame; and it's going to get worse. "There's an overwhelming consensus among scientists," said UW climate researcher David Battisti, who also was dubious about early claims of greenhouse warming.

Yet the message doesn't seem to be getting through to the public and policy-makers. Oklahoma Sen[ator] James Inhofe, chairman of the Senate Environment and Public Works Committee, calls global warming "the greatest hoax ever perpetuated on the American people." Novelist Michael Crichton's *State of Fear* landed on the best-seller list . . . [in 2005], by depicting global warming as a scare tactic of diabolical tree-huggers. A Gallup Poll in June [2005] found only about half of Americans believe the effects of global warming have already started. At the G8 summit of world leaders . . . [in 2005] President [George W.] Bush acknowledged man is warming the planet. But he stood alone in opposition to mandatory emissions controls, which he called too costly. "There's a huge disconnect between what professional scientists have studied and learned in the last 30 years, and what is out there in the popular culture," said Naomi Oreskes, a science historian at the University of California, San Diego.

Fuel companies contribute to that gap by supporting a small cadre of global-warming skeptics, whose views are widely disseminated by like-minded think tanks and Web sites. Most scientists don't know how to communicate their complex results to the public. Others are scared off by the shrill political debate over the issue. So their work goes on largely unseen, and largely pointing toward a warmer future.

The Consensus

Oreskes decided to quantify the extent of scientific agreement after a conversation with her hairdresser, who said she doesn't worry about global warming because scientists don't know what's going on. "That made me wonder why there's this weird public perception of what's been happening in climate science," Oreskes said. She analyzed 1,000 research papers on climate change selected randomly from those published between 1993 and 2003. The results were surprising: Not a single study explicitly rejected the idea that people are warming the planet. That doesn't mean there aren't any. But it does mean the number must be small, since none showed up in a sample that represents about 10 percent of the body of research, Oreskes said.

The consensus is most clearly embodied in the reports of the 100-nation Intergovernmental Panel on Climate Change (IPCC), established by the United Nations in 1988. Every five to six years, the panel evaluates the science and issues voluminous reports reviewed by more than 2,000 scientists and every member government, including the United States. The early reports reflected the squishy state of the science, but by 2001, the conclusion was unequivocal: "There is new and stronger evidence that most of the warming observed over the last 50 years is attributable to human activities."

In the history of science, no subject has been as meticulously reviewed and debated as global warming.

Stunned by the strong language, the Bush administration asked the prestigious National Academy of Sciences to evaluate the international group's work. . . . [University of Washington scientist John M.] Wallace served on the academy's panel, which assured the president the IPCC wasn't exaggerating. . . .

In the history of science, no subject has been as meticulously reviewed and debated as global warming, said science historian Spencer Weart, author of *The Discovery of Global Warming* [2004] and director of the Center for History of Physics. "The most important thing to realize is that most scientists didn't originally believe in global warming," he said. "They were dragged—reluctant step by step—by the facts."

A Reluctant Convert

Few were more reluctant converts than Wallace. A self-described weather nut who built a backyard meteorology station as a kid, he has spent his career trying to understand how the atmosphere behaves on a grand scale. By analyzing a decade of global climate records, Wallace was among the first to recognize El Niño's effects in the Pacific Northwest. He was recruited to the UW's [University of Washington's] fledgling meteorology program in 1966 and has helped build it into one of the world's top centers for atmospheric and ocean research.

His first foray into climate change came in the early 1990s after Russian friends told him deer carcasses stored in their "Siberian freezer"—the porch—were thawing out. Some scientists blamed global warming. Wallace examined the meteorological records and concluded natural wind shifts were blowing milder ocean air across the land. He briefly thought he had debunked global warming. Then he realized winds could account for only a small fraction of the warming in the planet's northernmost reaches, where average temperatures have now risen between 5 and 8 degrees in the past 50 years. "It was an evolution in my thinking," said Wallace, 64. "Like it or not, I could see global warming was going to become quite a big issue."

Global average air temperatures have risen about 1.2 degrees over the past century.

That's pretty much how the science of global warming has progressed. Researchers skeptical of the idea have suggested alternative causes for rising temperatures and carbon-dioxide levels. They've theorized about natural forces that might mitigate the effects of greenhouse gases. But no one has been able to explain it away. "You would need to develop a Rube Goldberg-type of argument to say climate is not changing because of increasing carbon dioxide," said [David] Battisti, 49, who directs the UW's Earth Initiative to apply science to environmental problems.

Global average air temperatures have risen about 1.2 degrees over the past century. The warming is also apparent in the oceans, in boreholes sunk deep in the ground, in thawing tundra and vanishing glaciers. Earth's climate has swung from steamy to icy many times in the past, but scientists believe they know what triggered many of those fluctuations. Erupting volcanoes and slow ocean upwelling release carbon dioxide, which leads to warming. Mountain uplifting and continental drift expose new rock, which absorbs carbon dioxide and causes cooling. Periodic wobbles in the planet's orbit reduce sunlight and set off a feedback loop that results in ice ages. All of those shifts happened over tens of thousands of years—and science shows none of them is happening now.

If greenhouse emissions continue unchecked, temperatures would likely be higher by the end of the century than any time since the human species evolved.

Instead, atmospheric levels of carbon dioxide are increasing at a rate that precisely tracks man's automotive and industrial emissions. "The process is 1,000 times faster than nature can do it," Battisti said. Climate reconstructions show that average global temperatures for the past 2 million years have never been more than 2 to 4 degrees higher than now. That means if greenhouse emissions continued unchecked, temperatures would likely be higher by the end of the century than any time since the human species evolved.

Skeptics Often Dominate Discussion

Eric Steig looks for answers about global warming in some of the Earth's most frigid spots. His walk-in freezers at the University of Washington are stacked with boxed ice cores from Antarctica and Greenland kept so cold he wears a parka and gloves to retrieve them. Steig, a geochemist, analyzes air bubbles and isotopes in the ice to reconstruct past temperatures and carbon-dioxide levels. He planned a career in physics until an undergraduate field project on the Juneau glacier fields kindled his passion for snow and ice. At 39, he belongs to a generation of climate researchers more open to global warming than the older guard, including Wallace and Battisti. Steig is also more frustrated by the way a handful of skeptics has dominated public debate. "Many of us have felt our voices are drowned out by the very well-funded industry viewpoint."

He and several colleagues set out this year to bridge the gap between science and popular perception with a Web log called RealClimate.org. Researchers communicate directly with the public and debunk what they see as misinformation and misconceptions. By giving equal coverage to skeptics on the fringe of legitimate science, journalists fuel the perception that the field is racked with disagreement. "You get the impression it's 50-50, when it's really 99-to-1," Steig said.

Over the past decade, coal and oil interests have funneled more than $1 million to about a dozen individual global-warming skeptics as part of an effort to "reposition global warming as theory rather than fact," according to industry memos first uncovered by former *Boston Globe* journalist Ross Gelbspan. From 2001 to 2003, ExxonMobil donated more than $6.5 million to organizations that attack mainstream climate science and oppose greenhouse-gas controls. These think tanks and advocacy groups issue reports, sponsor briefings and maintain Web sites that reach a far wider audience than scholarly climate journals.

Of course, there's nothing wrong with business questioning whether global-warming science justifies actions that may have profound economic impacts. And science can't advance without an open exchange of ideas. But climate researchers say skeptics are recycling discredited arguments or selectively using data to make points. And as Oreskes showed, few skeptics publish in peer-reviewed journals, which check for accuracy and omissions.

Industry Funds Some Skeptics

Oregon State climatologist George Taylor is a featured author on the Web site Tech Central Station, funded by Exxon and other corporations and described as the place where "free markets meet technology." He has a master's degree in meteorology and runs a state office based at Oregon State University [OSU] that compiles weather data and supplies it to policymakers, farmers and other customers. Taylor is not a member of OSU's academic faculty and has no published research on Arctic climate, but Sen[ator] Inhofe cited Taylor's claim that Arctic temperatures were much warmer in the 1930s as proof global warming is bogus.

James Overland, a Seattle-based oceanographer who has studied the Arctic for nearly 40 years, analyzed temperatures across a wider area than Taylor. His conclusion: The 1930s were warm—but the 1990s were warmer. Two other peer-reviewed analyses agree. Even more significant, Overland found the 1930s warming was typical of natural climate variation: Siberia might be warm one year and normal the next, while another part of the Arctic experienced unusual heat. Now there's persistent warming everywhere.

Taylor said in an e-mail that Tech Central Station paid him $500 for global-warming articles. United for Jobs, an industry coalition that opposes higher fuel-efficiency standards and greenhouse-gas limits, also paid Taylor and a co-author $4,000 for an article published on Tech Central Station. Mainstream climate scientists, including Wallace, Steig and Battisti, generally get their research money from the federal government. That doesn't make them immune from bias, said Patrick Michaels, one of the most widely quoted global-warming skeptics. Exaggerating the dangers of climate change can ensure a steady stream of money. "Global warming competes with cancer and competes with AIDS for a finite amount of money," said Michaels, a University of Virginia climatologist and fellow of the libertarian Cato Institute. "Nobody ever won that fight by saying: My issue isn't important." Michaels has received more than $165,000 in fuel-industry funding, including money from the coal industry to publish his own climate journal.

Skeptics portray themselves as Davids versus the Goliath of organized science, which is always resistant to new ideas. But global warming *is* the new idea, said Oreskes. Skeptics, she said, represent the old school of thought—that climate is so stable man could never tip it out of whack.

Climate Models Debated

Battisti planned to run his grandparents' dairy farm in upstate New York until a persistent professor nudged him toward science. A study on beach formation got him excited about hands-on oceanography, then he switched to atmospheric sciences in graduate school. He has analyzed some of the more cataclysmic climate-change scenarios, including the sudden shift depicted in the movie *The Day After Tomorrow*, and concluded they're highly unlikely.

These days, Battisti ponders the Eocene, a period 35 million to 50 million years ago when alligators lived near the Arctic Circle and palm trees grew in Wyoming. The world was hot because carbon-dioxide levels were three to five times higher than today—the result of a gradual buildup from volcanic eruptions. But global-climate computer models, which use mathematical formulas to represent complex atmospheric interactions, aren't able to reproduce that warming. When Battisti runs the models under Eocene-like conditions, they come up with much lower temperatures than actually existed—which means something was going on that scientists don't yet understand.

Models have improved greatly in the past 30 years but still can't anticipate all the ways the atmosphere will respond as greenhouse gases climb. The dozen models in use today predict average temperature increases of 3 to 11 degrees by the end of the century. Though the numbers sound modest, it took only a 10-degree drop to encase much of North America in mile-deep glaciers during the ice age that ended about 12,000 years ago.

Skeptics point to uncertainties in the models and conclude the actual temperature changes will be lower than the predictions. Battisti points to the Eocene and warns that unknown factors could just as easily make things worse. Could the skeptics be right, and the majority of the world's experts wrong? The history of science shows consensus doesn't guarantee success. The collective wisdom of the early 1900s declared continental drift bunk. Some Nobel laureates attacked Einstein's theory of relativity. Those blunders occurred when science was less sophisticated and connected than it is now, said Weart, the historian. With the unprecedented study devoted to climate change, the odds that this consensus is wrong are slim, he added. "The fact that so many scientists think it's likely a truck is heading for us means that the last thing we want to do is close our eyes and lie down in the road."

The United Nations Says the Evidence on Global Warming Is Unequivocal

Environment News Service

Environment News Service *is a daily international wire service covering issues on the environment.*

Changes in the atmosphere, the oceans, glaciers and ice caps show unequivocally that the Earth is warming, according to the first global assessment of climate change science in six years. The report confirms that the observed increase in atmospheric concentrations of greenhouse gases carbon dioxide, methane, and nitrous oxide since 1750 is the result of human activities. The [United Nations] Intergovernmental Panel on Climate Change, IPCC, concludes that advances in climate modeling and the collection and analysis of data now give scientists 90 percent confidence in their understanding of how human activities are causing the world to warm.

Greater Confidence

This level of confidence is much greater than what could be achieved in 2001 when the IPCC issued its last assessment. Introducing the report today [February 2, 2007] in Paris, Dr. Susan Solomon, an American atmospheric chemist, said it is "very likely," a 90 percent probability, that most of the observed increase in temperatures is due to the observed increase in greenhouse gas concentrations. The 2001 assessment said it was "likely," a probability of 66 percent. The rapid rise in global concentrations of carbon dioxide, methane and nitrous oxide, all greenhouse gases, is so different from the patterns for thousands of years previous, "there is no doubt that increase is dominated by human activity," said Solomon, who helped to identify the mechanism that created the Antarctic ozone hole.

IPCC Chairman Dr. R.K. Pachauri of India called the entire process of preparing the document, the first of four to be released this year by the panel, "a unique example of science in the service of society." He said 600 authors from 40 countries worked on the report, which was then assessed by 600 reviewers. Over the past several days, the whole thing was discussed by 300 delegations from 113 countries meeting in Paris. "This is the strength of the IPCC process," said Dr. Pachauri. "The scientists provide the knowledge, this is discussed and adopted by governments. It provides credibility."

The Impact of Warmer Temperatures

The report describes an accelerating transition to a warmer world marked by more extreme temperatures, heat waves, new wind patterns, worsening drought in some regions, heavier precipitation in others, melting glaciers and Arctic ice, and rising global average sea levels. For the first time, the report provides evidence that the ice sheets of Antarctica and Greenland are losing mass and contributing to sea level rise. An even greater degree of warming would likely have occurred if emissions of pollution particles and other aerosols had not offset some of the impact of greenhouse gases, by reflecting sunlight back out to space, the scientists said.

Solomon said the concentrations of greenhouse gases already in the atmosphere will continue to warm the planet for centuries, even if humans stabilize emissions within the next 10 years.

"This report by the IPCC represents the most rigorous and comprehensive assessment possible of the current state of climate science and has considerably narrowed the uncertainties of the 2001 report," said Michel Jarraud, secretary general of the World Meteorological Organization, WMO. "While the conclusions are disturbing, decision makers are now armed with the latest facts and will be better able to respond to these realities," Jarraud said. "The speed with which melting ice sheets are raising sea levels is uncertain, but the report makes clear that sea levels will rise inexorably over the coming centuries. It is a question of when and how much, and not if," he said.

Many Asians will be turned into environmental refugees as rising sea levels claim their lands.

"In our daily lives we all respond urgently to dangers that are much less likely than climate change to affect the future of our children," said Achim Steiner, executive director of the United Nations Environment Programme, UNEP, which, together with the WMO, established the Intergovernmental Panel on Climate Change in 1988. "February 2nd will be remembered as the date when uncertainty was removed as to whether humans had anything to do with climate change on this planet," said Steiner. "We are looking for an unequivocal response from politicians. The evidence is on the table, we no longer have to debate that part of it."

"Nine thousand children will be born worldwide during this one hour press conference," said Steiner, and it differs where you are born. African children will be faced with new diseases, new droughts, may have to leave their homes because Africa may have 30 percent of its coastal infrastructure destroyed by sea level rise. Many Asians will be turned into environmental refugees as rising sea levels claim their lands, Steiner warned. "The implications of global warming over the coming decades for our industrial economy, water supplies, agriculture, biological diversity and even geopolitics are massive," he said.

A Reason for Action

"Momentum for action is building," Steiner said. "This new report should spur policymakers to get off the fence and put strong and effective policies in place to tackle greenhouse gas emissions."

A warming of about 0.2°C is projected for each of the next two decades.

The IPCC Working Group I report, "The Physical Science Basis," concludes that:

- If atmospheric concentrations of greenhouse gases double compared to preindustrial levels, this would "likely" cause an average warming of around 3°C (5.4°F), with a range of 2 to 4.5°C (3.6–8.1°F). For the first time, the IPCC is providing best estimates for the warming projected to result from particular increases in greenhouse gases that could occur after the 21st century, along with uncertainty ranges based on more comprehensive modeling.

- A greenhouse gas level of 650 parts per million (ppm) would "likely" warm the global climate by around 3.6°C, while 750 ppm would lead to a 4.3°C warming, 1,000 ppm to 5.5°C and 1,200 ppm to 6.3°C. Future greenhouse gas concentrations are difficult to predict and will depend on economic growth, new technologies and policies and other factors.

- The world's average surface temperature has increased by around 0.74°C over the past 100 years (1906–2005). This figure is higher than the 2001 report's 100-year estimate of 0.6°C due to the recent series of extremely warm years, with 11 of the last 12 years ranking among the 12 warmest years since modern records began around 1850. A warming of about 0.2°C is projected for each of the next two decades.

- The best estimates for sea-level rise due to ocean expansion and glacier melt by the end of the century (compared to 1989–1999 levels) have narrowed to 28–58 cm, versus 9–88 cm in the 2001 report, due to improved understanding.

- However, larger values of up to one meter (39 inches) by 2100 cannot be ruled out if ice sheets continue to melt as temperature rises. The last time the polar regions were significantly warmer than at present for an extended period, about 125,000 years ago, reductions in polar ice volume caused the sea level to rise by four to six meters.

- Sea ice is projected to shrink in both the Arctic and Antarctic regions. Large areas of the Arctic Ocean could lose year-round ice cover by the end of the 21st century if human emissions reach the higher end of current estimates. The extent of Arctic sea ice has already shrank by about 2.7 percent per decade since 1978, with the summer minimum declining by about 7.4 percent per decade.

- Snow cover has decreased in most regions, especially in spring. The maximum extent of frozen ground in the winter/spring season decreased by about 7 percent in the Northern Hemisphere over the latter half of the 20th century. The average freezing date for rivers and lakes in the Northern Hemisphere over the past 150 years has arrived later by some 5.8 days per century, while the average break-up date has arrived earlier by 6.5 days per century.

- It is "very likely" that precipitation will increase at high latitudes and "likely" it will decrease over most subtropical land regions. The pattern of these changes is similar to what has been observed during the 20th century.

- It is "very likely" that the upward trend in hot extremes and heat waves will continue. The duration and intensity of drought has increased over wider areas since the 1970s, particularly in the tropics and subtropics. The Sahel, the Mediterranean, southern Africa and parts of southern Asia have already become drier during the 20th century.

- The amounts of carbon dioxide and methane now in the atmosphere far exceed pre-industrial values going back 650,000 years. Concentrations of carbon dioxide have already risen from a pre-industrial level of 280 ppm to around 379 ppm in 2005, while methane concentrations have risen from 715 parts per billion (ppb) to 1,774 in 2005.

- A number of widely discussed uncertainties have been resolved. The temperature record of the lower atmosphere from satellite measurements has been reconciled with the ground-based record. Key remaining uncertainties involve the roles played by clouds, glaciers and ice caps, oceans, deforestation and other land-use change, and the linking of climate and biogeochemical cycles.

The Intergovernmental Panel on Climate Change does not conduct new research. Instead, its mandate is to make policy relevant assessments of the existing worldwide literature on the scientific, technical and socioeconomic aspects of climate change. Its reports have played a major role in inspiring governments to adopt and implement the United Nations Framework Convention on Climate Change and the Kyoto Protocol.

Global Warming Deniers Are Politically Motivated and Funded by Oil Corporations

Chris Mooney

Chris Mooney is a senior correspondent for the American Prospect, *a political magazine. He is also the author of* The Republican War on Science *and* Storm World: Hurricanes, Politics, and the Battle Over Global Warming.

There is overwhelming scientific consensus that greenhouse gases emitted by human activity are causing global average temperatures to rise. Conservative think tanks are trying to undermine this conclusion with a disinformation campaign employing "reports" designed to look like a counterbalance to peer-reviewed studies, skeptic propaganda masquerading as journalism, and [other] events. The think tanks provide both intellectual cover for those who reject what the best science currently tells us, and ammunition for conservative policymakers like Senator James Inhofe (R-Okla.), the chair of the Environment and Public Works Committee, who calls global warming "a hoax."

This concerted effort reflects the shared convictions of free-market, and thus antiregulatory, conservatives. But there's another factor at play. In addition to being supported by like-minded individuals and ideologically sympathetic foundations, these groups are funded by ExxonMobil, the world's largest oil company. *Mother Jones* has tallied some 40 ExxonMobil-funded organizations that either have sought to undermine mainstream scientific findings on global climate change or have maintained affiliations with a small group of "skeptic" scientists who continue to do so. Beyond think tanks,

Chris Mooney, "Some Like It Hot," *Mother Jones*, vol. 30, May/June 2005, p. 36. www .motherjones.com. Copyright © 2005 Foundation for National Progress. Reproduced by permission.

the count also includes quasi-journalistic outlets like Tech CentralStation.com (a website providing "news, analysis, research, and commentary" that received $95,000 from ExxonMobil in 2003), a *FoxNews.com* columnist, and even religious and civil rights groups. In total, these organizations received more than $8 million between 2000 and 2003 (the last year for which records are available; all figures below are for that range unless otherwise noted). ExxonMobil chairman and CEO Lee Raymond serves as vice chairman of the board of trustees for the AEI [American Enterprise Institute], which received $960,000 in funding from ExxonMobil. The AEI-Brookings Institution Joint Center for Regulatory Studies . . . received another $55,000. . . .

ExxonMobil's Defense

Thirty years ago, the notion that corporations ought to sponsor think tanks that directly support their own political goals—rather than merely fund disinterested research—was far more controversial. But then, in 1977, an associate of the AEI came to industry's rescue. In an essay published in the *Wall Street Journal*, the influential neoconservative Irving Kristol memorably counseled that "corporate philanthropy should not be, and cannot be, disinterested," but should serve as a means "to shape or reshape the climate of public opinion." Kristol's advice was heeded, and today many businesses give to public policy groups that support a laissez-faire, antiregulatory agenda. In its giving report, ExxonMobil says it supports public policy groups that are "dedicated to researching free market solutions to policy problems." What the company doesn't say is that beyond merely challenging the Kyoto Protocol [an international treaty on global warming] or the McCain-Lieberman Climate Stewardship Act [an environment bill that was defeated in 2003] on *economic* grounds, many of these groups explicitly dispute *the science* of climate change. Generally eschewing peer-reviewed journals, these groups make their challenges in far less stringent arenas, such as the media and public forums.

No company appears to be working harder [than Exxon-Mobil] to support those who debunk global warming.

Pressed on this point, spokeswoman Lauren Kerr says that "ExxonMobil has been quite transparent and vocal regarding the fact that we, as do multiple organizations and respected institutions and researchers, believe that the scientific evidence on greenhouse gas emissions remains inconclusive and that studies must continue." She also hastens to point out that ExxonMobil generously supports university research programs—for example, the company plans to donate $100 million to Stanford University's Global Climate and Energy Project. It even funds the hallowed National Academy of Sciences.

Nevertheless, no company appears to be working harder to support those who debunk global warming. "Many corporations have funded, you know, dribs and drabs here and there, but I would be surprised to learn that there was a bigger one than Exxon," explains [Myron] Ebell of the Competitive Enterprise Institute [CEI], which, in 2000 and again in 2003, sued the government to stop the dissemination of a Clinton-era report showing the impact of climate change in the United States. Attorney Christopher Horner . . . was the lead attorney in both lawsuits and is paid a $60,000 annual consulting fee by the CEI. In 2002, ExxonMobil explicitly earmarked $60,000 for the CEI for "legal activities."

Ebell denies the sum indicates any sort of quid pro quo. He's proud of ExxonMobil's funding and wishes "we could attract more from other companies." He stresses that the CEI solicits funding for general project areas rather than to carry out specific sponsor requests, but admits being steered to the topics that garner grant money. While noting that the CEI is "adamantly opposed" to the Endangered Species Act, Ebell adds that "we are only working on it in a limited way now, because we couldn't attract funding."

ExxonMobil's funding of think tanks hardly compares with its lobbying expenditures—$55 million over the past six years, according to the Center for Public Integrity. And neither figure takes much of a bite out of the company's net earning—$25.3 billion last year. Nevertheless, "ideas lobbying" can have a powerful public policy effect. . . .

Industry Fights Back

To be sure, . . . science [on global warming] wasn't always as strong as it is today [June 2005]. And until fairly recently, virtually the entire fossil fuels industry—automakers, utilities, coal companies, even railroads—joined ExxonMobil in challenging it. The concept of global warming didn't enter the public consciousness until the 1980s. During a sweltering summer in 1988, pioneering NASA climatologist James Hansen famously told Congress he believed with "99 percent confidence" that a long-term warming trend had begun, probably caused by the greenhouse effect. As environmentalists and some in Congress began to call for reduced emissions from the burning of fossil fuels, industry fought back.

In 1989, the petroleum and automotive industries and the National Association of Manufacturers forged the Global Climate Coalition to oppose mandatory actions to address global warming. Exxon—later ExxonMobil—was a leading member, as was the American Petroleum Institute, a trade organization for which Exxon's CEO Lee Raymond has twice served as chairman. "They were a strong player in the Global Climate Coalition [GCC], as were many other sectors of the economy," says former GCC spokesman Frank Maisano.

Drawing upon a cadre of skeptic scientists, during the early and mid-1990s the GCC sought to emphasize the uncertainties of climate science and attack the mathematical models used to project future climate changes. The group and its proxies challenged the need for action on global warming, called the phenomenon natural rather than man-made, and even flatly denied it was happening. Maisano insists, however, that after the Kyoto Protocol emerged in 1997, the group focused its energies on making economic arguments rather than challenging science.

Many Industries Converted

Even as industry mobilized the forces of skepticism, however, an international scientific collaboration emerged that would change the terms of the debate forever. In 1988, under the auspices of the United Nations, scientists and government officials inaugurated the Intergovernmental Panel on Climate Change (IPCC), a global scientific body that would eventually pull together thousands of experts to evaluate the issue, becoming the gold standard of climate science. In the IPCC's first assessment report, published in 1990, the science remained open to reasonable doubt. But the IPCC's second report, completed in 1995, concluded that amid purely natural factors shaping the climate, humankind's distinctive fingerprint was evident. And with the release of the IPCC's third assessment in 2001, a strong consensus had emerged: Notwithstanding some role for natural variability, human-created greenhouse gas emissions could, if left unchecked, ramp up global average temperatures by as much as 5.8 degrees Celsius (or 10.4 degrees Fahrenheit) by the year 2100. "Consensus as strong as the one that has developed around this topic is rare in science," wrote *Science* Editor-in-Chief Donald Kennedy in a 2001 editorial.

Even some leading corporations that had previously supported "skepticism" were converted. Major oil companies like Shell, Texaco, and British Petroleum, as well as automobile manufacturers like Ford, General Motors, and Daimler-

Chrysler, abandoned the Global Climate Coalition, which itself became inactive after 2002.

Yet some forces of denial—most notably ExxonMobil and
the American Petroleum Institute [API], of which ExxonMobil
is a leading member—remained recalcitrant. In 1998, the *New
York Times* exposed an API memo outlining a strategy to invest millions to "maximize the impact of scientific views consistent with ours with Congress, the media and other key au-
diences." The document stated: "Victory will be achieved when
. . . recognition of uncertainty becomes part of the 'conventional wisdom.'" It's hard to resist a comparison with a famous Brown and Williamson tobacco company memo from
the late 1960s, which observed: "Doubt is our product since it
is the best means of competing with the 'body of fact' that exists in the mind of the general public. It is also the means of
establishing a controversy." . . .

Discrediting Science

Recently, Naomi Oreskes, a science historian at the University
of California at San Diego, reviewed nearly a thousand scientific papers on global climate change published between 1993
and 2003, and was unable to find one that explicitly disagreed
with the consensus view that humans are contributing to the
phenomenon. As Oreskes hastens to add, that doesn't mean
no such studies exist. But given the size of her sample, about
10 percent of the papers published on the topic, she thinks it's
safe to assume that the number is "vanishingly small."

What do the conservative think tanks do when faced with
such an obstacle? For one, they tend to puff up debates far beyond their scientific significance. A case study is the "controversy" over the work of University of Virginia climate scientist
Michael Mann. Drawing upon the work of several independent teams of scientists, including Mann and his colleagues,
the Intergovernmental Panel on Climate Change's 2001 report
asserted that "the increase in temperature in the 20th century

is likely to have been the largest of any century during the past 1,000 years." This statement was followed by a graph, based on one of the Mann group's studies, showing relatively modest temperature variations over the past thousand years and a dramatic spike upward in the 20th century. Due to its appearance, this famous graph has been dubbed the "hockey stick." . . .

A whole cottage industry has sprung up to criticize this analysis, much of it linked to ExxonMobil-funded think tanks. At a recent congressional briefing sponsored by the Marshall Institute, Senator Inhofe described Mann's work as the "primary scientific data" on which the IPCC's 2001 conclusions were based. That is simply incorrect. Mann points out that he's hardly the only scientist to produce a "hockey stick" graph—other teams of scientists have come up with similar reconstructions of past temperatures. And even if Mann's work and all of the other studies that served as the basis for the IPCC's statement on the temperature record are wrong, that would not in any way invalidate the conclusion that humans are *currently* causing rising temperatures. "There's a whole independent line of evidence, some of it very basic physics," explains Mann. Nevertheless, the ideological allies of ExxonMobil virulently attack Mann's work, as if discrediting him would somehow put global warming concerns to rest. . . .

There Is No Scientific Consensus on Global Warming

Lawrence Solomon

Lawrence Solomon is the executive director of Urban Renaissance Institute and Consumer Policy Institute, divisions of Energy Probe Research Foundation, a Canadian think tank.

"Only an insignificant fraction of scientists deny the global warming crisis. The time for debate is over. The science is settled." So said Al Gore . . . in 1992. Amazingly, he made his claims despite much evidence of their falsity. A Gallup poll at the time reported that 53% of scientists actively involved in global climate research did not believe global warming had occurred; 30% weren't sure; and only 17% believed global warming had begun. Even a Greenpeace poll showed 47% of climatologists didn't think a runaway greenhouse effect was imminent; only 36% thought it possible and a mere 13% thought it probable.

Today [June 2007], Al Gore is making the same claims of a scientific consensus, as do the United Nations' Intergovernmental Panel on Climate Change [IPCC] and hundreds of government agencies and environmental groups around the world. But the claims of a scientific consensus remain unsubstantiated. They have only become louder and more frequent.

No Consensus

More than six months ago, I began writing this series, *The Deniers*. When I began, I accepted the prevailing view that scientists overwhelmingly believe that climate change threatens the

Lawrence Solomon, "They Call This a Consensus?" *Financial Post*, June 2, 2007. www.canada.com/nationalpost/financialpost. Reproduced by permission.

planet. I doubted only claims that the dissenters were either kooks on the margins of science or sell-outs in the pockets of the oil companies.

Certainly there is no consensus [on global warming] at the very top echelons of scientists.

My series set out to profile the dissenters—those who deny that the science is settled on climate change—and to have their views heard. To demonstrate that dissent is credible, I chose high-ranking scientists at the world's premier scientific establishments. I considered stopping after writing six profiles, thinking I had made my point, but continued the series due to feedback from readers. I next planned to stop writing after 10 profiles, then 12, but the feedback increased. Now, after profiling more than 20 deniers, I do not know when I will stop—the list of distinguished scientists who question the IPCC grows daily, as does the number of emails I receive, many from scientists who express gratitude for my series.

Somewhere along the way, I stopped believing that a scientific consensus exists on climate change. Certainly there is no consensus at the very top echelons of scientists—the ranks from which I have been drawing my subjects—and certainly there is no consensus among astrophysicists and other solar scientists, several of whom I have profiled. If anything, the majority view among these subsets of the scientific community may run in the opposite direction. Not only do most of my interviewees either discount or disparage the conventional wisdom as represented by the IPCC, many say their peers generally consider it to have little or no credibility. In one case, a top scientist told me that, to his knowledge, no respected scientist in his field accepts the IPCC position.

Weaknesses in the IPCC Position

What of the one claim that we hear over and over again, that 2,000 or 2,500 of the world's top scientists endorse the IPCC position? I asked the IPCC for their names, to gauge their views. "The 2,500 or so scientists you are referring to are reviewers from countries all over the world," the IPCC Secretariat responded. "The list with their names and contacts will be attached to future IPCC publications, which will hopefully be on-line in the second half of 2007."

An IPCC reviewer does not assess the IPCC's comprehensive findings. He might only review one small part of one study that later becomes one small input to the published IPCC report. Far from endorsing the IPCC reports, some reviewers, offended at what they considered a sham review process, have demanded that the IPCC remove their names from the list of reviewers. One even threatened legal action when the IPCC refused.

A great many scientists, without doubt, are four-square in their support of the IPCC. A great many others are not. A petition organized by the Oregon Institute of Science and Medicine between 1999 and 2001 claimed some 17,800 scientists in opposition to the Kyoto Protocol. A more recent indicator comes from the U.S.-based National Registry of Environmental Professionals, an accrediting organization whose 12,000 environmental practitioners have standing with U.S. government agencies such as the Environmental Protection Agency and the Department of Energy. In a November 2006, survey of its members, it found that only 59% think human activities are largely responsible for the warming that has occurred, and only 39% make their priority the curbing of carbon emissions. And 71% believe the increase in hurricanes is likely natural, not easily attributed to human activities.

Such diversity of views is also present in the wider scientific community, as seen in the World Federation of Scientists, an organization formed during the Cold War to encourage dialogue among scientists to prevent nuclear catastrophe. The federation, which encompasses many of the world's most eminent scientists and today represents more than 10,000 scientists, now focuses on 15 "planetary emergencies," among them water, soil, food, medicine and biotechnology, and climatic changes. Within climatic changes, there are eight priorities, one being "Possible human influences on climate and on atmospheric composition and chemistry (e.g., increased greenhouse gases and tropospheric ozone)." Man-made global warming deserves study, the World Federation of Scientists believes, but so do other serious climatic concerns. So do 14 other planetary emergencies. That seems about right.

Claims About Global Warming Are Based on Junk Science

Richard Lindzen

Richard Lindzen is Alfred P. Sloan Professor of Atmospheric Science at the Massachusetts Institute of Technology.

There have been repeated claims that . . . [2006's] hurricane activity was another sign of human-induced climate change. Everything from the heat wave in Paris to heavy snows in Buffalo has been blamed on people burning gasoline to fuel their cars, and coal and natural gas to heat, cool and electrify their homes. Yet how can a barely discernible, one-degree increase in the recorded global mean temperature since the late 19th century possibly gain public acceptance as the source of recent weather catastrophes? And how can it translate into unlikely claims about future catastrophes?

The answer has much to do with misunderstanding the science of climate, plus a willingness to debase climate science into a triangle of alarmism. Ambiguous scientific statements about climate are hyped by those with a vested interest in alarm, thus raising the political stakes for policy makers who provide funds for more science research to feed more alarm to increase the political stakes. After all, who puts money into science—whether for AIDS, or space, or climate—where there is nothing really alarming? Indeed, the success of climate alarmism can be counted in the increased federal spending on climate research from a few hundred million dollars pre-1990 to $1.7 billion today [April 2006]. It can also be seen in heightened spending on solar, wind, hydrogen, ethanol and clean coal technologies, as well as on other energy-investment decisions.

But there is a more sinister side to this feeding frenzy. Scientists who dissent from the alarmism have seen their grant funds disappear, their work derided, and themselves libeled as industry stooges, scientific hacks or worse. Consequently, lies about climate change gain credence even when they fly in the face of the science that supposedly is their basis.

Misconceptions About Climate Change

To understand the misconceptions perpetuated about climate science and the climate of intimidation, one needs to grasp some of the complex underlying scientific issues. First, let's start where there is agreement. The public, press and policy makers have been repeatedly told that three claims have widespread scientific support: Global temperature has risen about a degree since the late 19th century; levels of CO_2 in the atmosphere have increased by about 30% over the same period; and CO_2 should contribute to future warming. These claims are true. However, what the public fails to grasp is that the claims neither constitute support for alarm nor establish man's responsibility for the small amount of warming that has occurred. In fact, those who make the most outlandish claims of alarm are actually demonstrating skepticism of the very science they say supports them. It isn't just that the alarmists are trumpeting model results that we know must be wrong. It is that they are trumpeting catastrophes that couldn't happen *even if the models were right* as justifying costly policies to try to prevent global warming.

Many scientists have been cowed not merely by money but by fear.

If the models are correct, global warming reduces the temperature differences between the poles and the equator. When you have less difference in temperature, you have less excitation of extratropical storms, not more. And, in fact, model runs support this conclusion. Alarmists have drawn some support for increased claims of tropical storminess from a casual claim by Sir John Houghton of the U.N.'s [United Nations'] Intergovernmental Panel on Climate Change (IPCC) that a warmer world would have more evaporation, with latent heat providing more energy for disturbances. The problem with this is that the ability of evaporation to drive tropical storms relies not only on temperature but humidity as well, and calls for drier, less humid air. Claims for starkly higher temperatures are based upon there being more humidity, not less—hardly a case for more storminess with global warming.

Intimidation of Skeptical Scientists

So how is it that we don't have more scientists speaking up about this junk science? It's my belief that many scientists have been cowed not merely by money but by fear. An example: Earlier this year, Texas Rep. Joe Barton issued letters to paleoclimatologist Michael Mann and some of his co-authors seeking the details behind a taxpayer-funded analysis that claimed the 1990s were likely the warmest decade and 1998 the warmest year in the last millennium. Mr. Barton's concern was based on the fact that the IPCC had singled out Mr. Mann's work as a means to encourage policy makers to take action. And they did so before his work could be replicated and tested—a task made difficult because Mr. Mann, a key IPCC author, had refused to release the details for analysis. The scientific community's defense of Mr. Mann was, nonetheless, immediate and harsh. The president of the National Academy of Science—as well the American Meteorological Society and the American Geophysical Union—formally protested, saying that Rep. Barton's singling out of a scientist's work smacked of intimidation.

All of which starkly contrasts to the silence of the scientific community when anti-alarmists were in the crosshairs of then-Sen. Al Gore. In 1992, he ran two congressional hearings during which he tried to bully dissenting scientists, including myself, into changing our views and supporting his climate alarmism. Nor did the scientific community complain when Mr. Gore, as vice president, tried to enlist Ted Koppel in a witch hunt to discredit anti-alarmist scientists—a request that Mr. Koppel deemed publicly inappropriate. And they were mum when subsequent articles and books by Ross Gelbspan libelously labeled scientists who differed with Mr. Gore as stooges of the fossil-fuel industry.

There is a strange reluctance to actually find out how climate really behaves.

Sadly, this is only the tip of a non-melting iceberg. In Europe, Henk Tennekes was dismissed as research director of the Royal Dutch Meteorological Society after questioning the scientific underpinnings of global warming. Aksel Winn-Nielsen, former director of the U.N.'s World Meteorological Organization, was tarred by Bert Bolin, first head of the IPCC, as a tool of the coal industry for questioning climate alarmism. Respected Italian professors Alfonso Sutera and Antonio Speranza disappeared from the debate in 1991, apparently losing climate-research funding for raising questions.

And then there are the peculiar standards in place in scientific journals for articles submitted by those who raise questions about accepted climate wisdom. At *Science* and *Nature*, such papers are commonly refused without review as being without interest. However, even when such papers are published, standards shift. When I, with some colleagues at NASA, attempted to determine how clouds behave under varying temperatures, we discovered what we called an "Iris Effect," wherein upper-level cirrus clouds contracted with increased temperature, providing a very strong negative climate feedback sufficient to greatly reduce the response to increasing CO_2. Normally, criticism of papers appears in the form of letters to the journal to which the original authors can respond immediately. However, in this case (and others) a flurry of hastily prepared papers appeared, claiming errors in our study, with our responses delayed months and longer. The delay permitted our paper to be commonly referred to as "discredited." Indeed, there is a strange reluctance to actually find out how climate really behaves. In 2003, when the draft of the U.S. National Climate Plan urged a high priority for improving our knowledge of climate sensitivity, the National Research Council instead urged support to look at the *impacts* of the warming—not whether it would *actually happen*.

Alarm rather than genuine scientific curiosity, it appears, is essential to maintaining funding. And only the most senior scientists today can stand up against this alarmist gale, and defy the iron triangle of climate scientists, advocates and policy makers.

Current
CONTROVERSIES

CHAPTER 2

Is Global Warming Caused by Human Activities?

Chapter Preface

Much scientific research on global warming has been directed toward measuring rising global temperatures, assessing the link between human activities and changes in climate, and projecting the impact of these changes based on current warming trends. According to a 2007 report by the United Nations Intergovernmental Panel on Climate Change (IPCC), climate scientists around the world agree that past and anticipated future temperature increases—driven largely by humans' reliance on fossil fuels such as coal, oil, and gas—pose an urgent global problem and even threaten life on Earth. Climate models relied upon by IPCC scientists, however, may not take sufficiently into account another scientific discovery about the Earth's climate—"global dimming"—so scientists' already pessimistic projections about rising temperatures may be vastly underestimating the actual rate and severity of global warming.

Global dimming, which is observed generally by a paler blue sky, is a term that describes a decrease in the amount of solar energy reaching the Earth's surface. This effect was first studied by Gerry Stanhill, a British scientist working in Israel in the 1990s. Stanhill compared sunlight records from the 1950s with current ones and was surprised to find that solar radiation in Israel had decreased dramatically—by about 22 percent—during recent decades. He then reviewed sunlight records taken at different points around the world and found that this appeared to be a global phenomenon, with some regions experiencing more dimming than others. For example, sunlight had decreased by 10 percent in the United States, almost 30 percent in some parts of the former Soviet Union, and by 16 percent in some places in the United Kingdom. Overall, the worldwide amount of sunlight had dimmed by two to four percent. Stanhill published his global dimming research in 2001, but his findings were largely ignored until his results were confirmed by Australian scientists using "pan evaporation" records—a totally different method of estimating solar radiation.

Stanhill and other scientists believe that the cause of this reduction of sunlight is particulate air pollution—the tiny particles of soot, ash, and other solid pollutants that are released with polluting gases when fossil fuels are burned. The gases cause the warming greenhouse effect, whereas the particulates attach to vapor and reflect sunlight, cooling the Earth's atmosphere. Dimming is caused when particles attract water droplets and create polluted clouds: The polluted clouds are more reflective and thus reflect more of the sun's energy back into space, reducing the amount of sunlight reaching the planet's surface.

Contrails—the vapor from jets seen as white streaks in the sky—form polluted clouds and are another significant cause of sunlight reflection. Scientist David Travis was able to confirm this theory when U.S. planes were grounded during the days after the terrorist attacks on September 11, 2001. He measured the sudden drop in particulate air pollution and noted the darker blue sky. The findings regarding global dimming suggest that the size of measured pollution from gas emissions is being reduced by the contrary action of pollution from solid particulates. The interaction of two patterns suggested a more complex problem than was previously envisioned.

Air pollution has long been known to be a danger to human health, but scientists think that global dimming caused by this pollution is also responsible for serious climate fluctuations. Pollution may have caused changes in rainfall patterns, possibly causing the major droughts in sub-Saharan Africa in the 1970s and 1980s that resulted in widespread disease and sharply increased mortality rates, particularly in Ethiopia. Similarly, scientists worry that a similar effect caused by growing industrial pollution in China and other rapidly developing Asian countries may be disrupting Asian monsoons, which provide vital water supplies to almost half of the world's population.

Even worse, scientists are now concerned that global dimming may be masking the real degree of future global warming. More specifically, researchers say that reductions in air pollution to make the air cleaner for people to breathe may be fueling an even more serious environmental problem—increases in global temperatures. If this is the case, well-intentioned reductions in air pollution could cause global warming to soar to much higher levels than currently projected—perhaps as much as 10 degrees Celsius, or 18 degrees Fahrenheit, within the next century. Such a staggering temperature increase would destroy many plants and animals that humans depend on for food, medicine, and other products; destroy the world economy; and make many regions on the Earth uninhabitable for humans.

The significance of these new findings about global dimming, researchers say, is that humans must immediately begin to reduce all types of industrial pollution—not only the air pollution that causes global dimming, but also the greenhouse gas pollution that is causing global warming. Many people believe we may have finally reached the point where there is no choice but to stop polluting the Earth.

Nonetheless, a minority of scientists and commentators continue to dispute the claim that rising temperatures are caused by human activities. Various articles and books have been written asserting that the warming trend is being caused mainly by natural rather than human forces. The authors of the following viewpoints present the range of opinions in this very crucial scientific debate.

Leading Scientists Are Certain that Global Warming Is Caused by Human Activities

Lisa Bryant

Lisa Bryant is a reporter for the Voice of America, a multimedia broadcasting service funded by the U.S. government that reports international news in forty-four languages around the world.

Top climate scientists have warned that global warming is here, it's caused by human activity, and the impact including rising sea level could persist for centuries. That's the consensus announced by an authoritative UN group including scientists from 113 countries. . . .

A Tough Wake-up Call

More intense storms; rising sea levels and higher temperatures; people being forced to flee their homes because of changing weather patterns—the findings presented by the Intergovernmental Panel on Climate Change (IPCC) amounted to the toughest wake-up call aired to date by 2,500 of the world's leading climate scientists. U.N. Environment Program head Achim Steiner told reporters in Paris . . . [in February 2007] that the world can no longer afford to ignore global warming. "It shifts from doubting to having to act, even if the last element of certainty is not yet there," Steiner said. "I think anyone who would continue to risk inaction on the basis of evidence presented here will one day in the history books be considered irresponsible."

Humans need to act, Steiner and other experts say, because human activity is the principle cause of rising temperatures and their effects in recent decades. The report says our

Lisa Bryant, "U.N. Report Confirms Human Activity to Blame for Earth's Warming Climate," Voice of America, February 5, 2007. www.voanews.com.

use of fossil fuels like oil and gas, our agricultural activities, and the other ways we exploit our planet have all produced heat-trapping greenhouse gases. The panel's new report predicts that temperatures will continue to rise between 1.8 degrees and 4 degrees Fahrenheit in this century alone.

More worrying, those temperature rises will continue over the new few centuries—even if we take action to reduce our greenhouse gas emissions. Senior U.S. government scientist Susan Solomon co-chaired the panel that prepared the report. "In terms of direct observations of climate change, the key conclusion is that warming of the climate system is now unequivocal," she said. "And that's evident in observations in air and ocean temperatures, melting of snow and ice, rising of global mean sea level."

We have already seen more intense storms and hurricanes, and . . . we'll very likely see more of these dramatic weather patterns in future years.

The report updates a previous report, released in 2001. And the scientists noted this survey is based on numerous studies that have taken place since then, and a more solid scientific consensus on global warming. Six years ago, the IPCC said only that global warming was "very likely" caused by human activity. This time, the group says it's 90 percent confident that man is responsible for rises in global temperatures.

The study tried to predict what we can expect in the coming decades. Sea levels may rise between 18 and 58 centimeters by the end of the century. We have already seen more intense storms and hurricanes, and the report says we'll very likely see more of these dramatic weather patterns in future years.

How will this affect humans? Well, says the U.N.'s Steiner, that all depends on where you live. "If you're an African child born in 2007, it's likely that by the time you're 50 years old you may in fact be faced with new diseases, you may be faced with new droughts, events in your life. You may even have to leave the areas you live in because some projections show that Africa may have 30 percent of its coastal infrastructure affected by the end of this century as a result of sea level rise." And if you're born in South Asia, water may flood your home, and you may become an environmental refugee.

A Broad Consensus

But much of the report is cautious and scientific. It is a consensus document, drafted and edited by hundreds of scientists. Some environmentalists feared the process might water down its conclusions.

IPCC chairman Rajendra Pachauri says the broad consensus is what gives the findings their credibility. "This is the strength of the IPCC process—it's essentially the scientists, the experts who are the ones who assess and provide the knowledge. But it's something that's discussed and debated by governments. And since we accept everything by consensus, the implication is that whatever is finally accepted and approved has the stamp of acceptance of all the governments of the world."

There's no excuse . . . for the public to sit back and do nothing.

Some panel members, such as Susan Solomon, are also clearly reluctant to step out of their scientific role. This is her answer to one reporter, who asked her what message the report sends to politicians, and what should be done: "I can only give you something that's going to disappoint you sir— and that is that it's my personal, scientific approach to say that it's not my role to try to communicate what should be done. I believe that is a societal choice."

The report has already sparked calls for action. French President Jacques Chirac called Friday for an environmental and political revolution to save the planet. Washington was more cautious. White House official Sharon Hays called it a significant report that will be valuable to policy makers.

Eduard Toulouse, a climate change expert at World Wildlife Fund France, agrees the panel's findings give countries like the United States, which has yet to sign the Kyoto global warming protocol, no more excuses for inaction. "Now the scientific statements are very clear," he said. "It is not possible to argue anymore and to wait, because the scientists tell us we have to act very quickly to cut our emissions of greenhouse gases if we want to avoid dramatic climate change." Toulouse also says the European Union must push for cutting greenhouse gas emissions by 30 percent by 2020. The 27-member bloc is currently debating new steps to take.

Individuals can also make a difference, the UN's Steiner says, cutting their own emissions to levels way below those set by the Kyoto Protocol. There's no excuse, he says, for the public to sit back and do nothing.

Mounting Evidence Supports the View that Global Warming Is Caused by Human Activities

Andrea Thompson

Andrea Thompson is a staff writer for LiveScience, *a science Web site.*

From catastrophic sea level rise to jarring changes in local weather, humanity faces a potentially dangerous threat from the changes our own pollution has wrought on Earth's climate. But since nothing in science can ever be proven with 100 percent certainty, how is it that scientists can be so sure that we are the cause of global warming?

Humans Are the Culprits

For years, there has been clear scientific consensus that Earth's climate is heating up and that humans are the culprits behind the trend, says Naomi Oreskes, a historian of science at the University of California, San Diego.

A few years ago, she evaluated 928 scientific papers that dealt with global climate change and found that none disagreed about human-generated global warming. The results of her analysis were published in a 2004 essay in the journal *Science.*

And the [United Nations] Intergovernmental Panel on Climate Change (IPCC), the National Academy of Sciences and numerous other noted scientific organizations have issued statements that unequivocally endorse the idea of global warming and attribute it to human activities. "We're confident

Andrea Thompson, "Global Warming: How Do Scientists Know They're Not Wrong?" *LiveScience*, July 16, 2007. www.livescience.com. Reproduced by permission.

about what's going on," said climate scientist Gavin Schmidt of NASA's Goddard Institute of Space Science in New York.

Science can never truly "prove" a theory. Science simply arrives at the best explanation of how the world works.

But even if there is a consensus, how can scientists be so confident about a trend playing out over dozens of years in the grand scheme of the Earth's existence? How do they know they didn't miss something, or that there is not some other explanation for the world's warming? After all, there was once a scientific consensus that the Earth was flat. How can scientists prove their position?

Best Predictor Wins

Contrary to popular parlance, science can never truly "prove" a theory. Science simply arrives at the best explanation of how the world works. Global warming can no more be "proven" than the theory of continental drift, the theory of evolution or the concept that germs carry diseases. "All science is fallible," Oreskes told *LiveScience*. "Climate science shouldn't be expected to stand up to some fantasy standard that no science can live up to."

Instead, a variety of methods and standards are used to evaluate the viability of different scientific explanations and theories. One such standard is how well a theory predicts the outcome of an event, and climate change theory has proven to be a strong predictor. The effects of putting massive amounts of carbon dioxide in the air were predicted as long ago as the early 20th century by Swedish chemist Svante Arrhenius.

Noted oceanographer Roger Revelle's 1957 predictions that carbon dioxide would build up in the atmosphere and cause noticeable changes by the year 2000 have been borne out by numerous studies, as has Princeton climatologist Suki Manabe's 1980 prediction that the Earth's poles would be first to see the effects of global warming. Also in the 1980s, NASA climatologist James Hansen predicted with high accuracy what the global average temperature would be in 30 years' time (now the present day [2007]). Hansen's model predictions are "a shining example of a successful prediction in climate science," said climatologist Michael Mann of Pennsylvania State University.

Skeptics have often raised the question of whether . . . global warming may in fact be explained by natural variation or changes in solar radiation.

Schmidt says that predictions by those who doubted global warming have failed to come true. "Why don't you trust a psychic? Because their predictions are wrong," he told *Live-Science*. "The credibility goes to the side that gets these predictions right."

Mounting Evidence

Besides their successful predictions, climate scientists have been assembling a "body of evidence that has been growing significantly with each year," Mann said data from tree rings, ice cores and coral reefs taken with instrumental observations of air and ocean temperatures, sea ice melt and greenhouse gas concentrations have all emerged in support of climate change theory. "There are 20 different lines of evidence that the planet is warming," and the same goes for evidence that greenhouse gases are increasing in the atmosphere, Schmidt said. "All of these things are very incontrovertible."

But skeptics have often raised the question of whether these observations and effects attributed to global warming may in fact be explained by natural variation or changes in solar radiation hitting the Earth. Hurricane expert William Gray, of Colorado State University, told *Discover* magazine in a 2005 interview, "I'm not disputing that there has been global warming. There was a lot of global warming in the 1930s and '40s, and then there was a slight global cooling from the middle '40s to the early '70s. And there has been warming since the middle '70s, especially in the last 10 years. But this is natural, due to ocean circulation changes and other factors. It is not human induced."

One argument commonly used to cast doubt on the idea of global warming is the supposed predictions of an impending ice age by scientists in the 1970s.

Isaac Newton had something to say about all this: In his seminal *Principia Mathematica,* he noted that if separate data sets are best explained by one theory or idea, that explanation is most likely the true explanation. And studies have overwhelmingly shown that climate change scenarios in which greenhouse gases emitted from human activities cause global warming best explain the observed changes in Earth's climate, Mann said—models that use only natural variation can't account for the significant warming that has occurred in the last few decades.

Mythic Ice Age

One argument commonly used to cast doubt on the idea of global warming is the supposed predictions of an impending ice age by scientists in the 1970s. One might say: First the Earth was supposed to be getting colder; now scientists say it's getting hotter—how can we trust scientists if their predictions are so wishy-washy? Because the first prediction was never actually made. Rather, it's something of an urban climate myth. Mann says that this myth started from a "tiny grain of truth around which so much distortion and misinformation has been placed."

Scientists were well aware of the warming that could be caused by increasing greenhouse gases, both Mann and

Schmidt explained, but in the decades preceding the 1970s, aerosols, or air pollution, had been steadily increasing. These tiny particles tended to have a cooling effect in the atmosphere, and at the time, scientists were unsure who would win the climate-changing battle, aerosols or greenhouse gases. "It was unclear what direction the climate was going," Mann said.

But several popular media, such as *Newsweek*, ran articles that exaggerated what scientists had said about the potential of aerosols to cool the Earth. But the battle is now over, and greenhouse gases have won. "Human society has made a clear decision as to which direction [the climate] is going to go," Mann said.

Future Predictions

One of the remaining skeptics, is MIT [Massachusetts Institute of Technology] meteorologist Richard Lindzen. While he acknowledges the trends of rising temperatures and greenhouse gases, Lindzen expressed his doubt on man's culpability in the case and casts doubt on the dire predictions made by some climate models, in an April 2006 editorial for the *Wall Street Journal*. "What the public fails to grasp is that the claims neither constitute support for alarm nor establish man's responsibility for the small amount of warming that has occurred," Lindzen wrote.

Climate scientists have clearly met the burden of proof [on global warming] with the mounting evidence they've assembled.

To be sure, there is a certain degree of uncertainty involved in modeling and predicting future changes in the climate, but "you don't need to have a climate model to know that climate change is a problem," Oreskes said.

Climate scientists have clearly met the burden of proof with the mounting evidence they've assembled and the strong predictive power of global warming theory, Oreskes said—global warming is something to pay attention to.

Schmidt agrees. "All of these little things just reinforce the big picture," he said. "And the big picture is very worrying."

Conservatives Must Accept the Reality that Human Activities Cause Global Warming

Jim Manzi

Jim Manzi is the CEO of an applied-artificial-intelligence software company.

It is no longer possible, scientifically or politically, to deny that human activities have very likely increased global temperatures; what remains in dispute is the precise magnitude of the human impact. Conservatives should accept this reality—and move on to the question of what we should do about it. This would put us in a much better position to prevent a massive, counterproductive intervention in the U.S. economy.

The Facts About Global Warming

Let's start with the facts. Why should we believe that rising concentrations of CO_2 and other greenhouse gases are driving increases in global temperatures? Not because of liberal scaremongering, or the media's fixation on every unusual weather event that comes along, but simply because of the underlying physics.

CO_2 is a greenhouse gas, which is to say, it absorbs and redirects infrared radiation but not shorter-wavelength radiation. The sun constantly bombards our planet with a significant amount of high-energy radiation with short wavelengths. Some portion of this is temporarily absorbed by the land and oceans, where it does work moving electrons. This work consumes energy, so a significant portion of this radiation that is subsequently re-emitted by the Earth is lower-energy, longer-

Jim Manzi, "Game Plan: What Conservatives Should Do About Global Warming," *National Review*, vol. 59, iss. 11, June 25, 2007, p. 31.

wavelength infrared radiation. As this re-emitted radiation travels through the atmosphere on its way back to space, some of it is absorbed by CO_2 molecules and then redirected back toward the Earth. If you are skeptical of this, you are skeptical of the last 120 years of particle physics. All else equal, the more CO_2 molecules we have in the atmosphere, the hotter it gets.

The most important scientific debate is really about ... feedback effects [of global warming].

The key question is how much hotter. In a simplified model of the planet in which I posit no complexities created by things like water vapor, convection, clouds, trees, polar ice caps, and so on, it is pretty straightforward to estimate. But here's the problem: The Earth is nothing like that planet. Any change, including pumping out more CO_2, kicks off an incredibly complicated set of feedback effects. Some of these will tend to magnify the greenhouse-warming impact, and others will tend to reduce it. Famously, as the atmosphere heats up, polar ice caps tend to melt; this in turn causes further heating. On the other hand, more CO_2 should lead to faster plant growth; this pulls CO_2 out of the atmosphere and therefore reduces warming. The list of such potential effects is very long, and many of these feedback effects interact with one another. This is what makes forecasting the climate an excruciatingly difficult scientific problem. It is also why we should be very wary of any silver-bullet alternative theories (such as the one involving variations in solar radiation) that claim to account for the recent run-up in global temperatures.

The most important scientific debate is really about these feedback effects. Feedbacks are not merely details to be cleaned up in a picture that is fairly clear. The base impact of a doubling of CO_2 in the atmosphere with no feedback effects is on the order of 1°C, while the United Nations Intergovernmental

Panel on Climate Change (IPCC) consensus estimate of the impact of doubling CO_2 is about 3°C. The feedback effects dominate the prediction. As we've seen, however, feedback effects run in both directions. Feedback could easily dampen the net impact so it ends up being less than 1°C. In fact, the raw relationship between temperature increases and CO_2 over the past century supports that idea.

Over the past several decades, teams in multiple countries have launched ongoing projects to develop large computer models that simulate the behavior of the global climate in order to account for feedback effects. While these models are complex, they are still extremely simplistic as compared with the actual phenomenon of global climate. Models have successfully replicated historical climates, but no model has ever demonstrated that it can accurately predict the climate impact of CO_2 emissions over a period of many years or decades.

Global warming . . . has been a partisan issue rather than a purely scientific discussion for a long time.

Climate models generate useful projections for us to consider, but the reality is that nobody knows with meaningful precision how much warming we will experience under any emissions scenario. Global warming is a real risk, but its impact over the next century could plausibly range from negligible to severe.

How Big a Deal?

Global warming, of course, has been a partisan issue rather than a purely scientific discussion for a long time, and conservatives have painted themselves into a corner. Based on the reasonable expectation that admitting a problem would lead to a huge government power grab, those conservatives with access to the biggest megaphones have used scientific uncertainty to avoid the issue. That game is just about up, and they suddenly find themselves walking unprepared into the middle of a sophisticated scientific and economic conversation about how to deal with the problem. While some conservative think tanks have considered these issues seriously for some time, the public discussion has been conducted up until now largely among various liberal factions and has turned into a technical debate about the most efficient tax scheme for reducing carbon emissions.

Prior engagement on the topic would have enabled conservatives to have made more persuasively the case that a policy of rapid, aggressive emissions abatement would be a terrible idea. Even if we assume that current climate models are perfectly accurate, and we further ignore the gigantic practical problem that China and India—the dominant emitters of the 21st century—will almost certainly not go along, the core issue remains that the benefits are not remotely worth the costs.

The current IPCC consensus forecast is that, under fairly reasonable assumptions for world population and economic growth, global temperatures will rise by 2.8°C by the year 2100. According to a decades-long modeling project by the Yale School of Forestry & Environmental Studies and Department of Economics, this amount of warming should result in zero to very mild net average global economic costs through 2100. Importantly, these models predict large negative impacts in poorer areas closer to the equator. Russia, Canada, and much of Europe are projected to benefit. The U.S. and China are projected to experience roughly break-even net impacts.

Only if temperatures continued to grow well beyond this level would truly costly net-negative U.S. and global impacts begin to be felt in the 22nd and 23rd centuries. According to the most recent IPCC Summary for Policymakers, a 4°C increase in temperatures would cause total economic losses of 1 to 5 percent of global GDP. That's a lot of money, but it's hardly Armageddon.

Competing Scenarios

The most frequently discussed methods for forcing the reduction of carbon emissions, and thereby reducing projected global warming, involve a direct or indirect tax on carbon. The theory is that we will sacrifice wealth today by forcing the economy to make less efficient use of resources, but in return enjoy future benefits because we avoid some of the costs that would have been created by ongoing global warming. The problem for the advocates of rapid reduction of carbon emissions is that the projected benefit is not the avoidance of global destruction, but rather the avoidance of costs of about 3 percent of global GDP—and even this benefit will be enjoyed only hundreds of years in the future, by a much wealthier world. These benefits, even if we accepted them as certain, would justify only very mild abatement of carbon emissions today, which can much more productively be accomplished by technological improvements than by a new worldwide tax regime.

Precisely because this broad case for immediate, aggressive abatement of carbon emissions doesn't withstand scrutiny, advocates have now begun to focus on the possibility of more specific climate catastrophes, such as the shutdown of the Gulf Stream or the loss of the Greenland Ice Sheet. If we were to accept that any one of these events was imminent, it would be rational to make huge sacrifices right now in a last-ditch effort to avoid it or soften its impact.

Fortunately, no mainstream science makes any such prediction of impending disaster; worry about them amounts to no more than informed speculation. The current IPCC report is explicit about this when it says: "Abrupt climate changes, such as the collapse of the West Antarctic Ice Sheet, rapid loss of the Greenland Ice Sheet, or large-scale changes in ocean circulation systems, are not considered likely to occur in the 21st century, based on currently available model results." That said, the same humility that leads us to a sensible skepticism about the ability of climate models to predict the temperature centuries into the future must also logically lead us to accept that some of these more extreme negative scenarios are not impossible. It is not a "scientific fact" that any of these things will occur; it is not even a quantifiable probability; but there is some currently unquantifiable but (crudely speaking) very low chance that one of these will happen.

Advocates have developed rationales for rapid carbon abatement that are really more or less sophisticated restatements of the idea that these downside risks are so bad that we should pay almost any price to avoid almost any chance of their occurrence. This concept has been called, somewhat grandiosely, the Precautionary Principle. Once you get past all of the table-pounding, this is the crux of the argument for emissions abatement. It is an emotionally appealing political position, as it is easy to argue that we should avoid some consumption now to head off even a low-odds possibility of a disaster.

A much more sensible strategy to deal with climate risk would emphasize technology rather than taxes.

But this is to get lost in the world of single-issue advocates and become myopic about risk. We face lots of other unquantifiable threats of at least comparable realism and severity. A regional nuclear war in Central Asia, a global pandemic triggered by a modified version of the HIV virus, or a rogue state weaponizing genetic-engineering technology all come immediately to mind. Any of these could kill hundreds of millions of people. Scare stories are meant to be frightening, but we shouldn't become paralyzed by them.

The Smart Way

In the face of massive uncertainty on multiple fronts, the best strategy is almost always to hedge your bets and keep your options open. Wealth and technology are raw materials for options. The loss of economic and technological development that would be required to eliminate literally all theorized climate-change risk would cripple our ability to deal with virtually every other foreseeable and unforeseeable risk, not to mention our ability to lead productive and interesting lives in the meantime. The Precautionary Principle is a bottomless well of anxieties, but our resources are finite. It's possible to buy so much flood insurance that you can't afford fire insurance.

In fact, a much more sensible strategy to deal with climate risk would emphasize technology rather than taxes. A science-based approach would hedge by providing support for prediction, mitigation, and adaptation technologies.

Prediction. We should start with the development of better climate-prediction tools. The climate-modeling community has made real progress, but needs to mature rapidly if we are to use climate models as the basis for trillion-dollar decisions. Today, climate modeling shows all the classic symptoms of poor supervision of smart analysts, including: excessive analytical complexity driven by researcher interest rather than focus on task-at-hand; lack of rigorous validation studies; software-engineering quality standards more appropriate for exploratory research than for reliable predictions; lack of transparent data standards; and an over-weighting of investment in analysis, as opposed to data collection and validation. The federal government should redirect funding in this area to develop a better software-modeling process, in combination with networks of physical sensors that can provide early-warning systems for the most plausible of the potential catastrophic climate scenarios.

Mitigation. Our economy is on a long-term trajectory of decarbonization as it becomes less energy-intensive and as the relative prices of alternative energy sources continue to drop compared with the price of fossil fuels. Accelerating this process is valuable for many reasons other than those involving climate change. Development of tactical technologies, such as carbon sequestration and cleaner-burning engines, would enable us to invent lower-emissions production facilities, automobiles, and so forth in the U.S., and export this technology to countries like China and India, where it would make the biggest difference (as these countries build up basic infrastructure). Using U.S. or European technology to increase the energy-conversion efficiency of coal-fired Chinese power plants as they come on line over the next few decades is a decidedly non-sexy measure; but it's probably the single most important action we can take to reduce carbon emissions over the next century.

Adaptation. Adaptation should take center stage, as it is by far the most cost-effective means of addressing climate risk. We can reduce the climate impact of carbon that is emitted, often using such simple techniques as planting more trees or using more reflective paint. Prosaic efforts—such as developing strains of crops that grow better in slightly warmer temperatures, better buttresses for buildings, and more intelligent zoning codes for coastal areas—can dramatically reduce losses from temperature swings, hurricanes, and floods today, and also reduce vulnerability to any potential future problems caused by climate change.

Global Warming Is the Result of Natural Forces

Bob Carter

Bob Carter is a geologist engaged in paleoclimate research at James Cook University in Queensland, Australia.

For many years now, human-caused climate change has been viewed as a large and urgent problem. In truth, however, the biggest part of the problem is neither environmental nor scientific, but a self-created political fiasco. Consider the simple fact, drawn from the official temperature records of the Climate Research Unit at the University of East Anglia, that for the years 1998–2005 global average temperature did not increase (there was actually a slight decrease, though not at a rate that differs significantly from zero).

Yes, you did read that right. And also, yes, this eight-year period of temperature stasis did coincide with society's continued power station and SUV-inspired pumping of yet more carbon dioxide into the atmosphere.

Sophisticated Brainwashing

In response to these facts, a global warming devotee will chuckle and say "how silly to judge climate change over such a short period". Yet in the next breath, the same person will assure you that the 28-year-long period of warming which occurred between 1970 and 1998 constitutes a dangerous (and man-made) warming. Tosh. Our devotee will also pass by the curious additional facts that a period of similar warming occurred between 1918 and 1940, well prior to the greatest phase of world industrialisation, and that cooling occurred between

Bob Carter, "There IS a Problem with Global Warming . . . It Stopped in 1998," *Sunday Telegraph* (UK), April 9, 2006. www.telegraph.co.uk. Reproduced by permission.

1940 and 1965, at precisely the time that human emissions were increasing at their greatest rate.

Does something not strike you as odd here? That industrial carbon dioxide is not the primary cause of earth's recent decadal-scale temperature changes doesn't seem at all odd to many thousands of independent scientists. They have long appreciated—ever since the early 1990s, when the global warming bandwagon first started to roll behind the gravy train of the UN Inter-governmental Panel on Climate Change (IPCC)—that such short-term climate fluctuations are chiefly of natural origin. Yet the public appears to be largely convinced otherwise. How is this possible?

Since the early 1990s, the columns of many leading newspapers and magazines, worldwide, have carried an increasing stream of alarmist letters and articles on hypothetical, human-caused climate change. Each such alarmist article is larded with words such as "if", "might", "could", "probably", "perhaps", "expected", "projected" or "modelled"—and many involve such deep dreaming, or ignorance of scientific facts and principles, that they are akin to nonsense.

Scientists are under intense pressure to conform with the prevailing paradigm of climate alarmism if they wish to receive funding for their research.

The problem here is not that of climate change per se, but rather that of the sophisticated scientific brainwashing that has been inflicted on the public, bureaucrats and politicians alike. Governments generally choose not to receive policy advice on climate from independent scientists. Rather, they seek guidance from their own self-interested science bureaucracies and senior advisers, or from the IPCC itself. No matter how accurate it may be, cautious and politically non-correct science advice is not welcomed in Westminster [the London seat of government in the U.K.], and nor is it widely reported.

Marketed under the imprimatur of the IPCC, the bladder-trembling and now infamous hockey-stick diagram that shows accelerating warming during the 20th century—a statistical construct by scientist Michael Mann and co-workers from mostly tree ring records—has been a seminal image of the climate scaremongering campaign. Thanks to the work of a Canadian statistician, Stephen McIntyre, and others, this graph is now known to be deeply flawed.

Intimidation of Dissenting Scientists

There are other reasons, too, why the public hears so little in detail from those scientists who approach climate change issues rationally, the so-called climate sceptics. Most are to do with intimidation against speaking out, which operates intensely on several parallel fronts.

First, most government scientists are gagged from making public comment on contentious issues, their employing organisations instead making use of public relations experts to craft carefully tailored, frisbee-science press releases. Second, scientists are under intense pressure to conform with the prevailing paradigm of climate alarmism if they wish to receive funding for their research. Third, members of the Establishment have spoken declamatory words on the issue, and the kingdom's subjects are expected to listen.

The reality of the climate record is that a sudden natural cooling is far more to be feared ... than the late 20th century phase of gentle warming.

On the alarmist campaign trail, the UK's [United Kingdom's] Chief Scientific Adviser, Sir David King, is thus reported as saying that global warming is so bad that Antarctica is likely to be the world's only habitable continent by the end of this century. Warming devotee and former Chairman of Shell, Lord [Ron] Oxburgh, reportedly agrees with another rash statement of King's, that climate change is a bigger threat than terrorism. And goodly Archbishop Rowan Williams, who self-evidently understands little about the science, has warned of "millions, billions" of deaths as a result of global warming and threatened Mr Blair [the British prime minister in 2006] with the wrath of the climate God unless he acts. By betraying the public's trust in their positions of influence, so do the great and good become the small and silly.

Fluctuations in Climate Change

Two simple graphs provide needed context, and exemplify the dynamic, fluctuating nature of climate change. The first is a temperature curve for the last six million years, which shows a three-million year period when it was several degrees warmer than today, followed by a three-million year cooling trend which was accompanied by an increase in the magnitude of the pervasive, higher frequency, cold and warm climate cycles. During the last three such warm (interglacial) periods, temperatures at high latitudes were as much as 5 degrees warmer than today's. The second graph shows the average global temperature over the last eight years, which has proved to be a period of stasis.

The essence of the issue is this. Climate changes naturally all the time, partly in predictable cycles, and partly in unpredictable shorter rhythms and rapid episodic shifts, some of the causes of which remain unknown. We are fortunate that our modern societies have developed during the last 10,000 years of benignly warm, interglacial climate. But for more than 90 per cent of the last two million years, the climate has been colder, and generally much colder, than today. The reality of the climate record is that a sudden natural cooling is far more to be feared, and will do infinitely more social and economic damage, than the late 20th century phase of gentle warming.

Sunspots and Cosmic Rays May Contribute to Climate Change

Peter N. Spotts

Peter N. Spotts is a staff writer for the Christian Science Monitor, *a daily newspaper published in Boston, Massachusetts.*

It's a modern-day climate scuffle William Herschel would recognize. He should. He helped trigger it.

In 1801, the eminent British astronomer reported that when sunspots dotted the sun's surface, grain prices fell. When sunspots waned, prices rose.

He suggested that shifts in grain prices were a stand-in for shifts in climate. Large numbers of sunspots led to a warmer sun, he reasoned. With more warmth reaching Earth, crop yields would increase, depressing grain prices.

Researchers [do not] doubt that over long time spans, changes in the level of sunlight reaching Earth's surface leave their imprints on climate.

With that, a 200-year hunt began for links between shifts in the sun's output and changes in climate.

No one doubts that the sun drives Earth's climate. Nor do researchers doubt that over long time spans, changes in the level of sunlight reaching Earth's surface leave their imprints on climate.

The vast bulk of research to date, however, points to greenhouse gases—mainly carbon dioxide from burning coal, oil, and natural gas—as the main force behind the current warming trend, most climate scientists say.

Still, over the past decade some researchers say they've found puzzling correlations between changes in the sun's output and weather and climate patterns on Earth. These links appear to rise above the level of misinterpreted data or faulty equipment.

"There are some empirical bits of evidence that show interesting relationships we don't fully understand," says Drew Shindell, a researcher at NASA's Goddard Institute for Space Studies in New York.

For example, he cites a 2001 study in which scientists looked at cloud cover over the United States from 1900 to 1987 and found that average cloud cover increased and decreased in step with the sun's 11-year sunspot cycle. The most plausible cause, they said: changes in the ultraviolet (UV) light the sun delivers to the stratosphere.

Clouds Can Cool, or Clouds Can Heat

Others claim to have linked shifts in levels of cosmic rays reaching deep into the atmosphere to changes in average cloud cover. Depending on how thick and how high they are, clouds either cool the planet by reflecting sunlight back into space or act as a blanket and trap heat. The valve controlling the flow of cosmic rays from deep space is the sun's magnetic field—which shifts with sunspot activity.

But this broad line of inquiry faces an enormous credibility problem, Dr. Shindell notes. From Herschel's day through the early 20th century, scientists have offered correlations that "fall apart the longer you look at them," he says.

Moreover, when scientists report a new correlation, some enthusiastic advocates go beyond what the data show and imbue it with too much significance. Such is the case with cosmic rays, many scientists say, whose poorly demonstrated ties to cloud formation have nevertheless been touted in the public arena—if not the scientific arena—as an explanation for most of the warming in the 20th century.

To say that current warming trends are "all cosmic rays and no carbon dioxide is totally ludicrous, in the same way that people say that it's all [human-induced] carbon dioxide and nothing natural. That is equally ludicrous," says Jasper Kirkby, a physicist who is actively exploring potential links between cosmic rays and clouds at CERN, Europe's center for high-energy physics research in Geneva.

"Climate is a cocktail," he explains. "The effect of cosmic rays on clouds—if there is a significant effect—will be part of the mix. The question is: Is it a significant part of the mix, or insignificant?"

Mainstream scientific skepticism about a strong direct link between changes in the sun's output and today's global warming stems from a tiny shift in sunlight.

Generally, peak periods of high sunspot activity deliver more sunlight to the top of the atmosphere than periods of minimum activity. Scientists measure this "total solar irradiance," which includes infrared and ultraviolet light as well as visible light.

In 1970, Russian researchers using high-altitude balloons to measure sunlight reported a 2 percent rise in the sun's output as the sun moved from periods of little sunspot activity to peak activity. Today, using better measurements from satellites over the past 28 years, the change in total solar irradiance is estimated to be much smaller, between 0.05 percent and 0.07 percent. The most important component for climate-change purposes—visible light—represents about half of this change, says Tom Woods, a researcher at the University of Colorado's Laboratory for Space and Atmospheric Physics, based in Boulder.

"Pesky" Correlations with Sunspots

Last fall [in 2006], solar physicists and climate scientists in the US and Europe reviewed the latest studies of changes in total solar irradiance driven by the 11-year sunspot cycle. They concluded that those changes are unlikely to have had a "significant influence" on global warming since the 1600s. In particular, satellite measurements since the late 1970s showed changes too weak to have "contributed appreciably to accelerated warming over the past 30 years."

The effect "is really small, unless you can come up with ways to amplify it," says Tom Wigley, a senior scientist at the National Center for Atmospheric Research in Boulder, who took part in the study.

Other studies suggest that changes in sunlight—as well as the cooling effect of volcanic activity, which sends sunlight-reflecting particles high in the sky—probably played a major role in climate during preindustrial times and even into the early 20th century. But even these find that CO_2 emissions have dominated the scene over the past half century.

Changes in solar UV output appear to redistribute warmth, chill, rainfall, and other conditions already present.

Some pesky correlations—such as the one between sunspot cycles and cloud cover—linger. This has led some scientists to ask if some process in the atmosphere may be boosting those tiny changes.

One candidate is UV light. During swings in sunspot cycles, the largest fractional changes in the sun's output occur in the ultraviolet range, Shindell notes. But much of that is absorbed by ozone in the stratosphere—which may be the connection, he suggests. The rise and fall of UV light can alter the amount of heat-trapping ozone in the stratosphere, changing its circulation patterns. These changes can work their way into the layer below, the troposphere, where weather and people meet. Instead of warming the troposphere, changes in solar UV output appear to redistribute warmth, chill, rainfall, and other conditions already present.

This mechanism may account for plunging winter temperatures in the Little Ice Age (1450 to 1850)—at least over land in the Northern Hemisphere, he says.

Another Possibility: Cosmic Rays

But if changes in ultraviolet light tied to sunspot cycles merely stir the climate pot, might something else affect long-term global average temperatures?

Enter galactic cosmic rays. In 1997, Danish researcher Henrik Svensmark and a colleague at the Danish Meteorological Institute injected new life into this debate with the first in a set of papers that suggested a strong correlation between an increase in galactic cosmic rays reaching Earth's surface during low points in the sunspot cycle and increased cloud cover.

The idea of a big effect on climate from cosmic rays is controversial. For instance, the team that studied sunspots and cloud cover over North America found that average cloudiness rose and fell with the sunspot cycle, but didn't track with cosmic ray trends.

Still, a study published last year in Britain showed a small but statistically significant effect from cosmic rays, notes Rasmus Benestad, who specialized in solar-climate interactions at the Norwegian Meteorological Institute in Oslo. He is highly skeptical that cosmic rays play a big role in climate, he says. But, he adds, the phenomenon is worth exploring.

Dr. Kirkby and colleagues at several institutions aim to do just that. They've designed an aerosol chamber to test how cosmic rays might affect cloud formation and how significant the effect might be. "You really can't settle the issue by more heated debate," he says. "You need experimental data."

Some Scientists Believe a Cooling Trend Is More Likely than Global Warming

Kate Ravilious

Kate Ravilious is a science writer based in York, England.

Simultaneous warming on Earth and Mars suggests that our planet's recent climate changes have a natural—and not a human-induced—cause, according to one scientist's controversial theory.

Warming on Mars

Earth is experiencing rapid warming, which the vast majority of climate scientists says is due to humans pumping huge amount of greenhouse gases into the atmosphere. Mars, too, appears to be enjoying more mild and balmy temperatures. In 2005 data from NASA's Mars Global Surveyor and Odyssey missions revealed that the carbon dioxide "ice caps" near Mars's south pole had been diminishing for three summers in a row.

Habibullo Abdussamatov, head of space research at St. Petersburg's Pulkovo Astronomical Observatory in Russia, says the Mars data is evidence that the current global warming on Earth is being caused by changes in the sun. "The long-term increase in solar irradiance is heating both Earth and Mars," he said.

Solar Cycle

Abdussamatov believes that changes in the sun's heat output can account for almost all the climate changes we see on both planets. Mars and Earth, for instance, have experienced peri-

Kate Ravilious, "Mars Melt Hints at Solar, Not Human, Cause for Warming, Scientist Says," *National Geographic News*, February 28, 2007. http://news.nationalgeogra phic.com. Reproduced by permission.

odic ice ages throughout their histories. "Man-made green-house warming has made a small contribution to the warming seen on Earth in recent years, but it cannot compete with the increase in solar irradiance," Abdussamatov said.

By studying fluctuations in the warmth of the sun, Abdus-samatov believes he can see a pattern that fits with the ups and downs in climate we see on Earth and Mars. Abdussamatov's work, however, has not been well received by other climate scientists. "His views are completely at odds with the mainstream scientific opinion," said Colin Wilson, a planetary physicist at England's Oxford University. "And they contradict the extensive evidence presented in the most recent IPCC [Intergovernmental Panel on Climate Change] report." Amato Evan, a climate scientist at the University of Wisconsin, Madison, added that "the idea just isn't supported by the theory or by the observations."

Planet's Wobbles

The conventional theory is that climate changes on Mars can be explained primarily by small alterations in the planet's or-bit and tilt, not by changes in the sun. "Wobbles in the orbit of Mars are the main cause of its climate change in the cur-rent era," Oxford's Wilson explained.

[Solar irradiance] "will cause a steep cooling of the cli-mate on Earth in 15 to 20 years."

All planets experience a few wobbles as they make their journey around the sun. Earth's wobbles are known as Mi-lankovitch cycles and occur on time scales of between 20,000 and 100,000 years. These fluctuations change the tilt of Earth's axis and its distance from the sun and are thought to be re-sponsible for the waxing and waning of ice ages on Earth. Mars and Earth wobble in different ways, and most scientists think it is pure coincidence that both planets are between ice ages right now. "Mars has no [large] moon, which makes its wobbles much larger, and hence the swings in climate are greater too," Wilson said.

No Greenhouse Effect

Perhaps the biggest stumbling block in Abdussamatov's theory is his dismissal of the greenhouse effect, in which atmospheric gases such as carbon dioxide help keep heat trapped near the planet's surface. He claims that carbon dioxide has only a small influence on Earth's climate and virtually no influence on Mars. But "without the greenhouse effect there would be very little, if any, life on Earth, since our planet would pretty much be a big ball of ice," said Evan, of the University of Wisconsin.

Most scientists now fear that the massive amount of carbon dioxide humans are pumping into the air will lead to a catastrophic rise in Earth's temperatures, dramatically raising sea levels as glaciers melt and leading to extreme weather worldwide. Abdussamatov remains contrarian, however, suggesting that the sun holds something quite different in store. "The solar irradiance began to drop in the 1990s, and a minimum will be reached by approximately 2040," Abdussamatov said. "It will cause a steep cooling of the climate on Earth in 15 to 20 years."

What Are the Potential Threats from Global Warming?

Chapter Preface

Many scientists predict that rising temperatures will create a highly volatile climate that will be characterized by more intense weather patterns, including stronger and more frequent hurricanes, windstorms, floods, fire, and drought. For insurance companies that insure against property losses caused by these types of natural catastrophes, global warming means higher risks, which will likely be passed on to the public, businesses, and governments in the form of higher insurance costs.

Hurricane Katrina, which struck the Gulf of Mexico in August 2005, was a wake-up call for the insurance industry and provided a compelling example of what a warmer future might bring. Until Katrina, the most costly natural catastrophe on record was Hurricane Andrew, which struck the United States in 1992 and cost the insurance industry around $20 billion. Experts say, however, that Katrina proved more than twice as costly as Andrew. Private insurance claims from the storm are expected to cost at least $56 billion, and some commentators have predicted the combined private and government costs of the hurricane could even reach as high as $200 billion.

If similar events were to happen frequently, experts say insurers could face worldwide losses totaling many hundreds of billions of dollars per year. Yet many people believe this is precisely what might occur. In fact, scientists say that climate change is already influencing the frequency and intensity of natural catastrophes. Major windstorms have set new loss records almost every year, and flood, drought, and forest fire emergencies tend to be more severe and seem to occur more frequently than ever before. Insurers find themselves paying out larger and larger amounts in compensation for losses, and the industry is beginning to consider what policy changes it should make to respond to this formidable business threat.

Despite the rising level of concern, however, most insurance companies do not yet factor the risks of general climate change into their catastrophe insurance premiums. Historically, the industry has based insurance rates on past claims and historical weather patterns, a practice that continues. Some industry leaders urge that this model be changed to account for the increased likelihood of future weather catastrophes, and some say this is already happening in an incremental way. As a result of more severe weather, for example, insurers have begun to charge higher premiums to homeowners and businesses located in coastal and other areas that have a high risk for hurricanes, floods, and fires. Some insurers have even withdrawn from these high-risk areas, refusing to offer insurance to people living in these places.

In the United States, for example, following Hurricane Katrina, major insurers won regulatory approval to raise rates in states hit by the storm, and many dropped policies or did not write new ones in coastal areas from Texas to Florida and up the East Coast as far as Massachusetts. People living in Midwestern flood zones and in western fire zones have also begun to experience difficulties getting home insurance. When new insurers enter these markets to provide insurance, their rates are often set much higher than in the past.

Insurers also have begun to grapple with other ways to respond to global warming. Some insurance experts, for example, say the industry needs to work with government to limit or upgrade construction in high-risk areas, in light of new weather patterns. Some insurers, too, are expected to lobby for stronger government action to limit greenhouse gases, invest in alternative energies, and combat global warming.

Still other companies have sought to hedge their increasing losses due to global warming by purchasing catastrophe bonds and weather derivatives—financial contracts between private parties that provide financial coverage for specific weather risks. For example, an insurance company might enter into a contract predicting a certain number of storms during a hurricane season as a way to hedge the risk of losses when homeowners lose their homes. Such a contract ends after that number of storms has occurred, theoretically blunting the company's potential losses in a worst-case scenario of catastrophic losses, but the company sacrifices the amount paid for the contract if the storm season is milder than expected. These hedge contracts are often funded by private investors willing to withstand high risks.

Weather changes, catastrophic property damages, and rising insurance costs, however, are only a small part of the threats posed by global warming. Experts say rising global temperatures could also cause significant environmental degradation, the extinction of many plant and animal species, food shortages, disease, and increased warfare. Indeed, some commentators warn that if the warming trend continues, planet Earth some day may not be able to support human life. The selections in this chapter address some of the more serious impacts of climate change.

Global Warming Will Have Severe Effects on the Environment in All Regions of the World

Jürg Rohrer

Jürg Rohrer is a graduate in engineering from the Technical University in Zürich, Switzerland, and has been a self-employed entrepreneur in the fields of environmental technology and IT.

An IPCC ([United Nations] Intergovernmental Panel on Climate Change) report including an update on predicted effects of global warming by geographical regions has been released in April 2007. This report does confirm the cause and effects of global warming, which have already been known for years. Further below we summarize the effects of global warming by geographical area (Africa, Asia, Australia and New Zealand, Europe, Latin America, North America, polar regions, small islands). The source of the data is the summary for policymakers of the report "Climate 2007" provided by IPCC.

Consequences of Global Warming

The report urges mankind to start acting quickly. But even very rigorous measures to reduce the emissions of greenhouse gases can only mitigate severe effects on our environment. Among the general consequences of global warming are:

- Increasing number of deaths as a consequence of heat waves, floods, droughts, tornadoes and other extreme weather conditions.

- More and larger fires in woods.

Jürg Rohrer, "Effects of Global Warming by Region (IPCC)," *Time for Change*, http://timeforchange.org. Reproduced by permission.

- Within a couple of decades, hundreds of millions of people will not have enough water.

- Reduction of the biological diversity on Earth: 20 to 30 percent of all species are expected to be extinguished. This will have severe consequences on the respective food chains.

- The increase of the sea level is expected to force tens of millions of people per year to move away from coastal areas within the next decades.

- Melting of glaciers: Small glaciers will disappear entirely, larger ones will shrink to about 30% of their current size.

- Change in agricultural yields will force many people (in particular for warmer countries) to migrate into other areas of the world. Hundreds of millions of people are facing starvation by the year 2080 as an effect of global warming.

- Comeback of diseases like malaria into areas, where they have previously been extinguished.

Expected Effects of Global Warming on Australia and New Zealand

- As a result of reduced precipitation and increased evaporation, water security problems are projected to intensify by 2030 in southern and eastern Australia and, in New Zealand, in Northland and some eastern regions.

- Significant loss of biodiversity is projected to occur by 2020 in some ecologically rich sites including the Great Barrier Reef and Queensland Wet Tropics. Other sites at risk include Kakadu wetlands, south-west Australia, sub-Antarctic islands and the alpine areas of both countries.

- Ongoing coastal development and population growth in areas such as Cairns and Southeast Queensland (Australia) and Northland to Bay of Plenty (New Zealand), are projected to exacerbate risks from sea-level rise and increases in the severity and frequency of storms and coastal flooding by 2050.

- Production from agriculture and forestry by 2030 is projected to decline over much of southern and eastern Australia, and over parts of eastern New Zealand, due to increased drought and fire. However, in New Zealand, initial benefits to agriculture and forestry are projected in western and southern areas and close to major rivers due to a longer growing season, less frost and increased rainfall.

- The region has substantial adaptive capacity due to well-developed economies and scientific and technical capabilities, but there are considerable constraints to implementation and major challenges from changes in extreme events. Natural systems have limited adaptive capacity.

Expected Effects of Global Warming on North America

- Moderate climate change in the early decades of the century is projected to increase aggregate yields of rain-fed agriculture by 5–20%, but with important variability among regions. Major challenges are projected for crops that are near the warm end of their suitable range or depend on highly utilised water resources.

- Warming in western mountains is projected to cause decreased snowfall, more winter flooding, and reduced summer flows, exacerbating competition for over-allocated water resources.

- Disturbances from pests, diseases, and fire are projected to have increasing impacts on forests, with an extended period of high fire risk and large increases in area burned.

- Cities that currently experience heat waves are expected to be further challenged, by an increased number, intensity and duration of heat waves during the course of the century, with potential for adverse health impacts. The growing number of the elderly population is most at risk.

- Coastal communities and habitats will be increasingly stressed by climate change impacts interacting with development and pollution. Population growth and the rising value of infrastructure in coastal areas increase vulnerability to climate variability and future climate change, with losses projected to increase if the intensity of tropical storms increases. Current adaptation is uneven and readiness for increased exposure is low.

Expected Effects of Global Warming on Latin America

- By mid-century, increases in temperature and associated decreases in soil water are projected to lead to gradual replacement of tropical forest by savanna in eastern Amazonia. Semi-arid vegetation will tend to be replaced by arid-land vegetation. There is a risk of significant biodiversity loss through species extinction in many areas of tropical Latin America.

- In drier areas, climate change is expected to lead to salinisation and desertification of agricultural land.

- Productivity of some important crops are projected to decrease and livestock productivity to decline, with adverse consequences for food security. In temperate zones soybean yields are projected to increase.

- Sea-level rise is projected to cause increased risk of flooding in low-lying areas.

- Increases in sea surface temperature due to climate change are projected to have adverse effects on Mesoamerican coral reefs, and cause shifts in the location of southeast Pacific fish stocks.

- Changes in precipitation patterns and the disappearance of glaciers are projected to significantly affect water availability for human consumption, agriculture and energy generation.

- Some countries have made efforts to adapt, particularly through conservation of key ecosystems, early warning systems, risk management in agriculture, strategies for flood drought and coastal management, and disease surveillance systems. However, the effectiveness of these efforts is outweighed by: lack of basic information, observation and monitoring systems; lack of capacity building and appropriate political, institutional and technological frameworks; low income; and settlements in vulnerable areas, among others.

Expected Effects of Global Warming on Europe

For the first time, wide ranging impacts of changes in current climate have been documented: retreating glaciers, longer growing seasons, shift of species ranges, and health impacts due to a heat wave of unprecedented magnitude. The observed changes described above are consistent with those projected for future climate change.

- Nearly all European regions are anticipated to be negatively affected by some future impacts of climate change and these will pose challenges to many economic sectors. Climate change is expected to magnify regional differences in Europe's natural resources and assets. Negative impacts will include increased risk of inland flash floods, and more frequent coastal flooding and increased erosion (due to storminess and sealevel rise). The great majority of organisms and ecosystems will have difficulties adapting to climate change.

- Mountainous areas will face glacier retreat, reduced snow cover and winter tourism, and extensive species losses (in some areas up to 60% under high emission scenarios by 2080).

- In Southern Europe, climate change is projected to worsen conditions (high temperatures and drought) in a region already vulnerable to climate variability, and to reduce water availability, hydropower potential, summer tourism, and in general, crop productivity. It is also projected to increase health risks due to heat waves and the frequency of wildfires.

- In Central and Eastern Europe, summer precipitation is projected to decrease, causing higher water stress. Health risks due to heat waves are projected to increase. Forest productivity is expected to decline and the frequency of peatland fires to increase.

- In Northern Europe, climate change is initially projected to bring mixed effects, including some benefits such as reduced demand for heating, increased crop yields and increased forest growth. However, as climate change continues, its negative impacts (including more frequent winter floods, endangered ecosystems and increasing ground instability) are likely to outweigh its benefits.

- Adaptation to climate change is likely to benefit from experience gained in reaction to extreme climate events, by specifically implementing proactive climate change risk management adaptation plans.

Expected Effects of Global Warming on Asia

- Glacier melt in the Himalayas is projected to increase flooding, rock avalanches from destabilised slopes, and affect water resources within the next two to three decades. This will be followed by decreased river flows as the glaciers recede.

- Freshwater availability in Central, South, East and Southeast Asia particularly in large river basins is projected to decrease due to climate change which, along with population growth and increasing demand arising from higher standards of living, could adversely affect more than a billion people by the 2050s.

- Coastal areas, especially heavily-populated mega-delta regions in South, East and Southeast Asia, will be at greatest risk due to increased flooding from the sea and in some mega-deltas flooding from the rivers.

- Climate change is projected to impinge on sustainable development of most developing countries of Asia as it compounds the pressures on natural resources and the environment associated with rapid urbanisation, industrialisation, and economic development.

- It is projected that crop yields could increase up to 20% in East and Southeast Asia while it could decrease up to 30% in Central and South Asia by the mid-21st century. Taken together and considering the influence of rapid population growth and urbanisation, the risk of hunger is projected to remain very high in several developing countries.

- Endemic morbidity and mortality due to diarrhoeal disease primarily associated with floods and droughts are expected to rise in East, South and Southeast Asia due to projected changes in hydrological cycle associ-

103

ated with global warming. Increases in coastal water temperature would exacerbate the abundance and/or toxicity of cholera in South Asia.

Expected Effects of Global Warming on Africa

- By 2020, between 75 and 250 million people are projected to be exposed to an increase of water stress due to climate change. If coupled with increased demand, this will adversely affect livelihoods and exacerbate water-related problems.

- Agricultural production, including access to food, in many African countries and regions is projected to be severely compromised by climate variability and change. The area suitable for agriculture, the length of growing seasons and yield potential, particularly along the margins of semi-arid and arid areas, are expected to decrease. This would further adversely affect food security and exacerbate malnutrition in the continent. In some countries, yields from rain-fed agriculture could be reduced by up to 50% by 2020.

- Local food supplies are projected to be negatively affected by decreasing fisheries resources in large lakes due to rising water temperatures, which may be exacerbated by continued over-fishing.

- Towards the end of the 21st century, projected sea-level rise will affect low-lying coastal areas with large populations. The cost of adaptation could amount to at least 5–10% of GDP. Mangroves and coral reefs are projected to be further degraded, with additional consequences for fisheries and tourism.

- New studies confirm that Africa is one of the most vulnerable continents to climate variability and change because of multiple stresses and low adaptive capacity. Some adaptation to current climate variability is taking place, however, this may be insufficient for future changes in climate.

Expected Effects of Global Warming on Small Islands

- Small islands, whether located in the Tropics or higher latitudes, have characteristics which make them especially vulnerable to the effects of climate change, sea level rise and extreme events.

- Deterioration in coastal conditions, for example through erosion of beaches and coral bleaching, is expected to affect local resources, e.g., fisheries, and reduce the value of these destinations for tourism.

- Sea-level rise is expected to exacerbate inundation, storm surge, erosion and other coastal hazards, thus threatening vital infrastructure, settlements and facilities that support the livelihood of island communities.

- Global warming is projected by the mid-century to reduce water resources in many small islands, e.g., in the Caribbean and Pacific, to the point where they become insufficient to meet demand during low rainfall periods.

- With higher temperatures, increased invasion by non-native species is expected to occur, particularly on middle and high-latitude islands.

Expected Effects of Global Warming on Polar Regions

- In the polar regions, the main projected biophysical effects are reductions in thickness and extent of glaciers and ice sheets, and changes in natural ecosystems with detrimental effects on many organisms including mi-gratory birds, mammals and higher predators. In the Arctic, additional impacts include reductions in the extent of sea ice and permafrost, increased coastal erosion, and an increase in the depth of permafrost seasonal thawing.

- For Arctic human communities, impacts, particularly resulting from changing snow and ice conditions, are projected to be mixed. Detrimental impacts would include those on infrastructure and traditional indigenous ways of life.

- Beneficial impacts would include reduced heating costs and more navigable northern sea routes.

- In both polar regions, specific ecosystems and habitats are projected to be vulnerable, as climatic barriers to species' invasions are lowered.

- Already Arctic human communities are adapting to climate change, but both external and internal stressors challenge their adaptive capacities. Despite the resilience shown historically by Arctic indigenous communities, some traditional ways of life are being threatened and substantial investments are needed to adapt or re-locate physical structures and communities. . . .

The true cause of global warming is our thoughtless attitude to Nature. We seem to have forgotten that we are only part of a larger whole. The bottom line is that we all will have to reduce our energy consumption down to a level which can be supplied by renewable energies. A sustainable living is the only long-term solution.

By 2050, Global Warming Could Cause the Extinction of More than a Million Species

Shaoni Bhattacharya

Shaoni Bhattacharya is a reporter for New Scientist, *an online science and technology news magazine.*

Global warming may drive a quarter of land animals and plants to the edge of extinction by 2050, a major international study has warned. In the worst-case scenario, between a third to a half of land animal and plant species will face extermination. The predictions come from extinction models based on over 1100 species covering a fifth of the Earth's land mass.

The bleak scenarios result from a study by Chris Thomas at the University of Leeds, UK [United Kingdom], and colleagues, who have evaluated the impact on species of mild, moderate and severe levels of predicted climate change. "The absolutely best-case scenario—which in my opinion is unrealistic—with the minimum expected climate change and all of the species moving completely into new areas which become suitable for them, means we end up with an estimate of nine per cent facing extinction," Thomas told *New Scientist*. This would mean about one million species would be doomed, assuming there are 10 million species in existence.

Solid and Sound

"The broad conclusions are very solid, and very sound, and very alarming," says Stuart Pimm, an expert in extinctions and biodiversity at Duke University, North Carolina, US. "It's a hugely important paper." Previous studies have looked at the

Shaoni Bhattacharya, "Global Warming Threatens Millions of Species," *NewScientist .com*, vol. 18, iss. 24, January 7, 2004. Copyright © 2004 Reed Elsevier Business Publishing, Ltd. Reproduced by permission.

effects of global warming on individual species. The new study is the most comprehensive analysis to date, bringing together simulation studies of where species may move in a warmer world.

To curb climate change, serious and immediate action must be implemented at the highest intergovernmental levels.

The news is "not very encouraging," Pimm told *New Scientist*. "It suggests that species' extinctions following on from global change will broadly be in the same order of magnitude as species lost due to habitat destruction." The World Conservation Union's Red Book lists between 10 and 30 per cent of species as endangered due to habitat loss.

Thomas says the effects of climate change should be considered as great a threat to biodiversity as the "Big Three"— habitat destruction, invasions by alien species and overexploitation by humans. He says the study overturns the notion that "climate change might simply result in the reassembling of species around the planet, without them dying out".

Representative Sample

Thomas and colleagues around the world statistically modelled the climates in which each of the 1103 species considered currently live. Whole groups of plant and animal species confined to a particular region, for example, the Amazon, were evaluated. Endangered species would have been included among these, as well as more common species, so Thomas says there is no reason to suppose that the organisms selected are unrepresentative of species generally.

The survival of each species was then modelled under the minimum, mid-range and maximum global warming scenarios predicted by the Intergovernmental Panel on Climate Change. Every species thrives best in certain conditions in-

volving factors such as temperature and rainfall. So, Thomas says, the question was then: "Where are these same conditions going to be found?" However, not all species would be physically able to migrate to new locations with equivalent conditions as the Earth heats up. And with lots of species, the models predicted that their new environment would be considerably smaller than their old habitats—a basic tenet of ecology is that smaller areas support fewer species. Using the mid-range climate predictions, the researchers found that by 2050 between 15 and 37 per cent of the species would be on the "slippery slope" to extinction.

Both Thomas and Pimm agree that to curb climate change, serious and immediate action must be implemented at the highest intergovernmental levels. This would include cutting emissions of greenhouse gases, employing new energy efficient technologies and using strategies to sequester carbon dioxide from the atmosphere.

Global Warming May Increase the Risk of Wildfires

Peter N. Spotts

Peter N. Spotts is a staff writer for the Christian Science Monitor, *a daily newspaper published in Boston, Massachusetts.*

Droughts, floods, severe storms, and sea-level rise often get the lion's share of attention in the litany of projected effects from global warming. But October's [2007] disastrous wildfires in California—part of one of the most intense fire seasons in the United States in nearly 50 years—are likely to raise the profile of such events, even if a firm link between the state's fires and climate change has yet to be made. . . .

Global warming is expected to increase fire hazards in the western United States under a range of global-warming scenarios. But the greatest increase in risk, some researchers say, is likely to come in the East and Southeast. There, snowmelt and rainfall are unlikely to slake the increasing thirst of trees and shrubs as CO_2 spurs their growth during longer, warmer growing seasons. This could leave more of the eastern woodlands drier and more vulnerable to wildfires by summer's end. Meanwhile, some of the most dense mingling of homes and woods—what experts call the wildland-urban interface—can be found in the eastern U.S. . . .

But pinning the blame for southern California's tragedy on global warming at this stage is premature, says Anthony Westerling, an assistant professor at the University of California at Merced and a lead investigator with the California Climate Change Center at the Scripps Institution of Oceanography in La Jolla, Calif.

He and colleagues at the University of Arizona note that so far no research has identified a clear link between rising temperatures and wildfires in southern California's dry chaparral landscape. In a statement, the team notes that "the connection between global warming, Santa Ana winds, and extremely low southern California precipitation last winter are not known with sufficient certainty to conclusively link global warming with this disaster."

Global warming's fingerprints—earlier springs, earlier snowmelts, and warmer temperatures—have been appearing in . . . forested areas.

"We don't know how much the dice are getting loaded" in favor of such fire outbreaks in southern California, Dr. Westerling says in an interview. Computer models tend to agree that temperatures should warm, he says, but "they are all over the place" on changes in precipitation.

Yet global warming's fingerprints—earlier springs, earlier snowmelts, and warmer temperatures—have been appearing in other forested areas, he adds. In a study he and colleagues published in the journal *Science* in August 2006, the team found a sudden, marked increase in the number and lifetime of fires, as well as a longer fire season in the West generally—especially during the mid-1980s. These trends were particularly noticeable in forests in the northern Rockies at middle elevations. There, the interaction of people with the forest ecosystem—which can have its own powerful effect on fires—is far less pronounced than in other parts of the West.

Indeed, model projections point to similar trends in Canada and Russia's immense reaches of high-latitude forests, according to a research by a team led by Amber Soja, a researcher at the National Aeronautics and Space Administration's Langley Research Center in Hampton, Va.

That global warming might bring a greater fire risk to the already arid Western U.S. might seem obvious. But the big surprise in the future may come farther east, says Ronald Neilson, a bioclimatologist at the U.S. Forest Service's Pacific Northwest Research Station in Portland, Ore. It's in the east and southeast where global-warming-related wildfire risks will grow the most dramatically, his research suggests, even though the western U.S. remains the country's wildfire hot spot.

Why? As temperatures warm, the growing season will get longer. Woodlands will grow faster—at least for a few decades—fertilized by more atmospheric CO_2. But annual precipitation amounts are expected to remain relatively constant.

Today, forests usually dry out just as the trees are going dormant for winter. In the future, however, eastern forests may dry long before the trees have a chance to shut down. Combined with bark beetle infestations (themselves a product of warming temperatures; they have occurred in the southern and western U.S. and recently moved east), an increasing number of eastern woodlands could become prime wildfire fuel.

Global Warming Will Likely Bring a Rise in Infectious Diseases

American Society for Microbiology

The American Society for Microbiology is a membership organization for scientists from around the world.

As the Earth's temperatures continue to rise, we can expect a significant change in infectious disease patterns around the globe. Just exactly what those changes will be remains unclear, but scientists agree they will not be for the good.

Unknown Effects

"Environmental changes have always been associated with the appearance of new diseases or the arrival of old diseases in new places. With more changes, we can expect more surprises," says Stephen Morse of Columbia University, speaking May 22, 2007, at the 107th General Meeting of the American Society for Microbiology in Toronto [Canada]. In its April 2007 report on the impacts of climate change, the Intergovernmental Panel on Climate Change (IPCC) warned that rising temperatures may result in "the altered spatial distribution of some infectious disease vectors," and will have "mixed effects." . . .

"Diseases carried by insects and ticks are likely to be affected by environmental changes because these creatures are themselves very sensitive to vegetation type, temperature, humidity, etc. However, the direction of change—whether the diseases will increase or decrease—is much more difficult to predict, because disease transmission involves many factors,

American Society for Microbiology, "Scientists Concerned About Effects of Global Warming on Infectious Diseases," *ScienceDaily*, May 23, 2007. www.sciencedaily.com. Reproduced by permission.

some of which will increase and some decrease with environmental change. A combination of historical disease records and present-day ground-based surveillance, remotely sensed (satellite) and other data, and good predictive models is needed to describe the past, explain the present and predict the future of vector-borne infectious diseases," says David Rogers of Oxford University, also speaking at the meeting.

More Malaria and Flu

One impact of rising global temperatures, though, can be fairly accurately predicted, says Morse. In the mountains of endemic areas, malaria is not transmitted above a certain altitude because temperatures are too cold to support mosquitoes. As temperatures rise, this malaria line will rise as well. "One of the first indicators of rising global temperatures could be malaria climbing mountains," says Morse.

Another change could be the flu season. Influenza is a year-round event in the tropics. If the tropical airmass around the Earth's equator expands, as new areas lose their seasons they may also begin to see influenza year-round.

More Disease in General

And extreme weather events will also lead to more disease, unless we are prepared. As the frequency, intensity, and duration of extreme weather events change, water supplies become more at risk, according Joan Rose of Michigan State University. "Hurricanes, typhoons, tornadoes and just high intensity storms have exacerbated an aging drinking and wastewater infrastructure, enhanced the mixing of untreated sewage and water supplies, re-suspended pathogens from sediments and displaced large populations to temporary shelters. We are at greater risk than ever before of infectious disease associated with increasing extreme weather events," says Rose. There will also be indirect effects of climate change on infectious disease as well. For instance, says Morse, the effect of global warming on agriculture could lead to significant changes in disease transmission and distribution.

"If agriculture in a particular area begins to fail due [to] drought, more people will move into cities," says Morse. High population densities, especially in developing countries, are associated with an increased transmission of a variety of diseases including HIV, tuberculosis, respiratory diseases (such as influenza) and sexually transmitted diseases. "I'm worried about climate change and agree that something needs to be done," says Morse. "Otherwise, we can hope our luck will hold out."

Global Warming May Cause Food Shortages

Martin Mittelstaedt

Martin Mittelstaedt is an environmental reporter for the Globe and Mail, *a nationally distributed, Canadian English-language newspaper based in Toronto, Canada.*

The place where most of the world's people could first begin to feel the consequences of global warming may come as a surprise: in the stomach, via the supper plate. That's the view of a small but influential group of agricultural experts who are increasingly worried that global warming will trigger food shortages long before it causes better known but more distant threats, such as rising sea levels that flood coastal cities.

The Impact on Wheat, Corn, and Rice

The scale of agriculture's vulnerability to global warming was highlighted late last year [2006] when the Consultative Group on International Agricultural Research (CGIAR), an umbrella organization representing 15 of the world's top crop research centres, issued an astounding estimate of the impact of climate change on a single crop, wheat, in one of the world's major breadbaskets.

Researchers using computer models to simulate the weather patterns likely to exist around 2050 found that the best wheat-growing land in the wide arc of fertile farmland stretching from Pakistan through Northern India and Nepal to Bangladesh would be decimated. Much of the area would become too hot and dry for the crop, placing the food supply of 200 million people at risk. "The impacts on agriculture in

Martin Mittelstaedt, "How Global Warming Goes Against the Grain," *The Globe and Mail*, February 23, 2007. www.theglobeandmail.com. Reprinted with permission from *The Globe and Mail*.

developing countries, and particularly on countries that depend on rain-fed agriculture, are likely to be devastating," says Dr. Louis Verchot, principal ecologist at the World Agroforestry Centre in Nairobi, Kenya.

Wheat, the source of one-fifth of the world's food, isn't the only crop that could be clobbered by climate change. Cereals and corn production in Africa are at risk, as is the rice crop in much of India and Southeast Asia, according to Dr. Verchot.

Agriculture is vulnerable to global warming because the world's most widely eaten grains—corn, wheat, and rice—are exquisitely sensitive to higher temperatures.

In a cruel twist of fate, most of the hunger resulting from global warming is likely to be felt by those who haven't caused the problem: the people in developing countries. At the same time, it may be a boon to agriculture in richer northern countries more responsible for the greenhouse gas emissions driving climate instability. "With climate change, the agricultural areas in Canada, Russia and Europe will expand, while the areas suited for agriculture in the tropics will decline," Dr. Verchot says. "Basically, the situation is that those who are well off now will be better off in the future, and those who are in problems will have greater problems."

The Rule of Temperature in Food Production

Agriculture is vulnerable to global warning because the world's most widely eaten grains—corn, wheat, and rice—are exquisitely sensitive to higher temperatures. In the tropics and subtropics, many crops are already being grown just under the maximum temperatures they can tolerate. Over the 10,000 years that humans have farmed, temperatures have been remarkably stable, at current levels or slightly cooler, and plants are finely attuned to this climate regimen.

Although it doesn't work exactly the same for each crop, a rough rule of thumb developed by crop scientists is that, for every 1-degree Celsius increase in temperatures above the mid-30s during key stages in the growing season, such as pollination, yields fall about 10 percent.

Average global temperatures will likely rise between 1.1 to 6.4 degrees over the next century, . . . suggesting that . . . crops will suffer problematic declines.

In the case of rice, researchers found the plants were most sensitive to higher nighttime temperatures. For crops in general, optimum growing conditions generally range from about 20 to 35 degrees, and then diminish sharply. At 40 degrees— temperatures that are now starting to occur in many areas— heat stress causes photosynthesis to shut down. Such high temperatures are starting to become more common, such as during the devastating heat wave in much of Europe in the summer of 2003 that killed tens of thousands.

Average global temperatures will likely rise between 1.1 to 6.4 degrees over the next century, according to the authoritative Intergovernmental Panel on Climate Change, suggesting that, over most of the range of future temperatures, crops will suffer problematic declines. The panel is also warning that global warming will alter rainfall patterns, causing increasing numbers of droughts and floods.

The threatened wheat-growing area around India is known as the Indo-Gangetic Plain. Summer temperatures already sometimes reach a sizzling 45 degrees [Celsius, or 113 degrees Fahrenheit] there, even though global warming is in its early days. Agricultural researchers with the CGIAR thought the decline in wheat-growing capacity of the plain, which includes the Punjab, was so worrisome they hurriedly made the finding public, although the full study in which it is described, called "Can Wheat Beat the Heat?" is not going to be released until later.

That such a fabled agricultural region—source of one-sixth of the global wheat crop—could be severely affected by rising temperatures holds symbolic importance, because the Indo-Gangetic Plain represents one of the world's most significant victories against food shortages. The area "really is the epicentre of the green revolution in the 1970s, where wheat and rice scientists saw the first big gains that were coming out of modern plant-breeding techniques," says Nathan Russell, a spokesman at the CGIAR, which is based in Washington. The worry is that climate change might "erase all of these gains," he says.

Grain Vulnerability

Perhaps the best-known worrier about climate change and its impact on agriculture is Lester Brown, founder of the Earth Policy Institute, a U.S. environmental think tank, and proponent of the view that global warming and agriculture are on a collision course. "It certainly looms large," Mr. Brown says of the threat posed to farming by a warmer world.

One of the solutions to global warming—using crops to produce clean-burning bio-fuels such as ethanol—would accentuate any harvest shortfalls.

Mr. Brown says the global food larder is already so bare that the impact of global warming could be felt at any time—even as early as this summer—if it causes rising temperatures or changing precipitation patterns that lead to a crop failure in any major agricultural region. The food surpluses of yesteryear have been nibbled down to the point where practically nothing is left in the bin for coping with even one disappointing harvest, he says. "The unfortunate reality is that the cushion for dealing with climate change now is less than it's been for 34 years, because in six out of the last seven years world grain production has fallen short of consumption."

Furthermore, one of the solutions to global warming—using crops to produce clean-burning bio-fuels such as ethanol—would accentuate any harvest shortfalls because so much corn, sugar, and soybeans is now being diverted from the dinner plate to the gas tank.

The Earth Policy Institute tracks the world's stockpile of grain—the amount available in storage after accounting for annual use and production—and says it's down to only 57 days of consumption. This is close to the modern nadir, a period in the early 1970s of poor harvests when levels fell so low there was only enough for 56 days. That earlier period of short supply prompted a doubling of world grain prices—an indication of the possible consequences if global warming takes a bite out of harvests.

Even North America's prime piece of agricultural real estate, the continent's equivalent of the Indo-Gangetic Plain, is in the gunsights of climate change. The models that simulate the likely effects of climate change show that the regions warming the most are at mid to high latitudes, and in mid-continental areas far from the moderating effects of oceans. "Those conditions sort of describe the U.S. corn belt and the Great Plains, the wheat-growing Great Plains of the U.S. and Canada," Mr. Brown says. "Since we are the world's bread basket, if we start losing wheat production and corn production, it's going to affect the entire world."

The study released by CGIAR did find that rising temperatures would cause a remarkable northward shift of the wheat belt. The crop could theoretically be cultivated in a band across the top of North America—from Cape Harrison, about midway up the coast of Labrador, to Ketchikan, on the Alaskan panhandle, in the west. But agricultural experts say don't bother hoping for northern regions to become replacement granaries for losses in the tropics. Trading the rich soils of the Punjab or the U.S. Midwest for the thin soils of Labrador and the north coast of Lake Superior, in other words, is a bit like a gambler discarding an ace for a two. It's probably an unwise bet. "The northward movement of a climate zone into an area where crops generally have not been grown does not necessarily mean crops like wheat will do well there," says Dr. Hans Braun, director of the global wheat program at CIMMYT, the Mexico-based crop research institute that conducted the wheat study.

No Benefit to Greenhouse Gases

Scientists have made another worrisome discovery, this time about carbon dioxide itself, the main greenhouse gas, which is vital for plant development. It had been assumed in the 1980s, based on greenhouse experiments, that an atmosphere richer in carbon dioxide would stimulate plant growth, raising some crop yields by as much as 30 per cent. That is part of the reason why, up until now, few people worried much about agriculture and global warming. It was thought that, while climate change might wreak havoc on ice-dependent polar bears and low-lying coastal cities, it held a verdant lining for farmers.

But new research published last year [2006] based on experiments in the U.S., Japan, Switzerland and New Zealand found the beneficial effects of carbon dioxide were vastly overrated when crops were grown in the more realistic setting of open farm fields, rather than in greenhouses. Corn yields didn't rise at all, and the rise in wheat and rice yields was less than half previous estimates.

Hope for Heat-resistant Plants

To be sure, not everyone is convinced that crop problems are inevitable. Donald Coxe, global portfolio strategist for BMO Financial Group, says plant breeders have made remarkable advances in producing crops more tolerant of extreme conditions. "It's quite amazing what they can do," he says.

Researchers . . . have called for a massive program to develop crops that will be able to cope with global warming.

Mr. Coxe, an investment adviser based in Chicago who follows the commodity markets, where prices would skyrocket if food shortages develop, says last year's corn harvest was a case in point. Illinois, at the heart of the U.S. corn belt, was sizzled by heat and drought, but many farmers still managed a decent crop thanks to seeds bred to give plants more resistance to drought. "Illinois was a shocker, frankly, last year, even to ag [agricultural] people. They were amazed," he says.

Researchers affiliated with CGIAR have called for a massive program to develop crops that will be able to cope with global warming, and these developments may well pan out. But if efforts fail, Mr. Brown, for one, is warning the consequences could be dire, because food supplies are essential for global stability. Smaller grain harvests will translate into sharply higher food prices. Soaring prices, says Mr. Brown, "could lead to urban food riots in scores of countries around the world, and those food riots could lead to political instability and that political instability could begin to undermine global economic progress."

Global Warming Could Cause Resource Wars

Brad Knickerbocker

Brad Knickerbocker is a staff writer for the Christian Science Monitor, *a daily newspaper published in Boston, Massachusetts.*

For years, the debate over global warming has focused on the three big "E's": environment, energy, and economic impact. . . . [In April 2007] it officially entered the realm of national security threats and avoiding wars as well. A platoon of retired US generals and admirals warned that global warming "presents significant national security challenges to the United States." The United Nations [UN] Security Council held its first ever debate on the impact of climate change on conflicts. And in Congress, a bipartisan bill would require a National Intelligence Estimate by all federal intelligence agencies to assess the security threats posed by global climate change.

A Threat Multiplier

Many experts view climate change as a "threat multiplier" that intensifies instability around the world by worsening water shortages, food insecurity, disease, and flooding that lead to forced migration. That's the thrust of a 35-page report by 11 admirals and generals this week issued by the Alexandria, Va.-based national security think tank the CNA Corporation. The study, titled National Security and the Threat of Climate Change, predicts:

> Projected climate change will seriously exacerbate already marginal living standards in many Asian, African, and

Brad Knickerbocker, "Could Global Warming Cause War? A New Report Warns That Conflicts Over Water and Food Could Intensify as the Climate Changes," *Christian Science Monitor*, April 19, 2007. Reproduced by permission from *Christian Science Monitor*, www.csmonitor.com.

Middle Eastern nations, causing widespread political instability and the likelihood of failed states.... The chaos that results can be an incubator of civil strife, genocide, and the growth of terrorism.

The U.S. may be drawn more frequently into these situations, either alone or with allies, to help provide stability before conditions worsen and are exploited by extremists. The U.S. may also be called upon to undertake stability and reconstruction efforts once a conflict has begun, to avert further disaster and reconstitute a stable environment.

"We will pay for this one way or another," retired Marine Gen. Anthony Zinni, former commander of American forces in the Middle East and one of the report's authors, told the Los Angeles *Times*. "We will pay to reduce greenhouse gas emissions today ... or we'll pay the price later in military terms. And that will involve human lives."

Many of the most severe effects of global warming are expected in regions where fragile governments are least capable of responding to them.

As quoted in *Associated Press*, British Foreign Secretary Margaret Beckett, who presided over the UN meeting in New York April 17, [2007], posed the question "What makes wars start?" The answer: "Fights over water. Changing patterns of rainfall. Fights over food production, land use. There are few greater potential threats to our economies ... but also to peace and security itself." This is the concern behind a recently introduced bipartisan bill by Sen[ator]s Richard Durbin (D) of Illinois and Chuck Hegel (R) of Nebraska. It would require all US intelligence agencies—the CIA [Central Intelligence Agency], the NSA [National Security Agency], the Pentagon, and the FBI [Federal Bureau of Investigation]—to conduct a comprehensive review of potential security threats related to climate change around the world.

"Many of the most severe effects of global warming are expected in regions where fragile governments are least capable of responding to them," Senator Durbin said in a story from the Inter Press Service news agency in Rome. "Failing to recognize and plan for the geopolitical consequence of global warming would be a serious mistake."

Rep. Edward J. Markey (D) of Massachusetts, chairman of the newly formed House Select Committee on Energy Independence and Global Warming, is proposing companion legislation that would fund climate change plans by the Department of Defense. On his website, Mr. Markey called for action based on the retired senior officers' report, saying: "Global warming's impacts on natural resources and climate systems may create the fiercest battle our world has ever seen. If we don't cut pollution and head off severe global warming at the pass, we could see extreme geopolitical strain over decreased clean water, environmental refugees, and other impacts."

Clean technology is going to create "massive" market opportunities.

In a speech April 16 [2007] to BritishAmerican Business Inc., a trans Atlantic business organization, British Foreign Secretary Beckett "praised the growing actions of US business executives and state politicians in addressing climate change, including California Governor Arnold Schwarzenegger, who along with British Prime Minister Tony Blair announced plans last year [2006] to work toward a possible joint emissions-trading market," reported the *Associated Press*.

Ms. Beckett also told the business executives that clean technology is going to create . . . "massive" market opportunities: "Those who move into that market first—first to design, first to patent, first to sell, first to invest, first to build a brand—have an unparalleled chance to make money."

Implications for National and International Security

The Bush administration has taken a less stark view of the security implications of greenhouse-gas emissions than many scientists and military offices. But in a broader context, the administration has agreed that environmental issues could present national and international security challenges. In its 2006 National Security Strategy the administration acknowledged that environmental destruction, including that caused by human activity, "may overwhelm the capacity of local authorities to respond, and may even overtax national militaries, requiring a larger international response. . . . These challenges are not traditional national security concerns, such as the conflict of arms or ideologies. But if left unaddressed they can threaten national security."

These concerns are likely to keep growing and continue to be on the agendas at international meetings. A strongly worded draft communique for June's [2007] G8 [a group of leading industrialized countries] summit in Heiligendamm, Germany, warns that "tackling climate change is an imperative, not a choice," reported the British newspaper *The Independent* on Sunday. The draft says: "Global warming caused largely by human activities is accelerating [and it] will seriously damage our common natural environment and severely weaken [the] global economy, with implications for international security."

Global Warming Could Make the Earth Unlivable for Humans

Dale Allen Pfeiffer

Dale Allen Pfeiffer is a geologist, science journalist, and author of The End of the Oil Age.

The possibility of runaway global warming is not as distant a threat as we may wish. It is a threat which worries some of the greatest minds living among us today. Stephen Hawking, physicist, best selling author of *A Brief History of Time*, and claimant of the Cambridge University post once occupied by Sir Isaac Newton (the Lucasian Chair of Mathematics), has been quoted as saying, "I am afraid the atmosphere might get hotter and hotter until it will be like Venus with boiling sulfuric acid." The renowned physicist was joined by other notables such as former President Jimmy Carter, former news anchor Walter Cronkite, and former astronaut and Senator John Glenn in drafting a letter to urge President Bush to develop a plan to reduce US emissions of greenhouse gases. Former British Environmental Minister Michael Meacher is also worried about the survival of the human race due to global warming....

Why do so many prominent people worry about runaway global warming? The fear is that, once the atmosphere has warmed past some critical level, various feedback mechanisms will kick in and push the temperature beyond the point where the planet will become inhospitable for human life. Once these feedback mechanisms have kicked in, it is unlikely that we can do anything to intervene. And considering the current signs from the environment, accelerating industrial emissions,

Dale Allen Pfeiffer, "Global Climate Change & Peak Oil (Part III)," *fromthewilderness.com*, 2004. Reproduced by permission.

and the long life of greenhouse gases in the atmosphere, some worry that it may already be too late to prevent this scenario.

Runaway Climate Change—Feedback Mechanisms

Many processes in the natural world have continuous consequences which either accelerate or retard the original process. Such consequences feed back into the process from which they arise, and so are called "feedback loops.". . .

Our climate system is largely a system of feedback mechanisms, both positive and negative. It is the crux of the climate change skeptics' argument that negative feedback systems will cancel out industry-induced global climate change. They suggest that excess carbon in the atmosphere will be absorbed by the oceans and will stimulate photosynthesis in land-based plants, both of which will serve to remove the excess carbon from the atmosphere and lock it safely away.

Currently [as of 2004], photosynthesis in forests is accelerating, leading to greener, lusher forests and a higher absorption rate for carbon dioxide. However, decomposition rates in dead wood and soils are also beginning to accelerate. And as the climate warms, eventually this outgassing of decomposed carbon will overtake the accelerated photosynthesis. Worse, the Amazonian rainforests are expected to fail about mid-century. The dying rainforests would then release their store of carbon into the atmosphere. According to studies undertaken by the Met Office Hadley Centre for Climate Prediction in Great Britain, if industrial carbon emissions go unmitigated then the forests will become net contributors of carbon to the atmosphere by 2070. Stabilization of industrial emissions could possibly delay this forest dieback for another century.

Ocean Carbon Feedback

Climate change skeptics point to the oceans as an immense carbon sink, capable of absorbing all industrial carbon emissions. Indeed, the oceans hold a volume of carbon equivalent to more than 6,000 years of fossil fuel burning at current rates. Without the absorption of carbon by the oceans and the linked production of free oxygen by ocean phytoplankton, the Earth's atmosphere would consist almost entirely of carbon dioxide, with a little bit of nitrogen. Temperatures would hover around 600° Celsius, and atmospheric pressure would be 60 times heavier than it is currently.

[The] oceanic carbon sink could very well break down in response to climate change.

Ocean waters absorb carbon dioxide from the atmosphere, holding much of it in solution, but transforming some into carbolic acid. Phytoplankton in the upper ocean layers fix the carbon dioxide in their cells through the process of photosynthesis. These phytoplankton form the basis of the ocean food chain. They are grazed by animal plankton and other organisms, which utilize most of the carbon as an energy source but return a small portion of it to the atmosphere through respiration. Some of this carbon ultimately settles through the ocean column in the form of cast-off tests and shells, and animal feces. During periods of global warming millions of years ago, this sediment of carbon wastes formed the source for the hydrocarbon deposits which have served to power our civilization through the past century, and which are now, ironically, resulting in industry-induced climate change.

Unfortunately, this oceanic carbon sink could very well break down in response to climate change. Warmer seawater is already saturated with carbon, so it absorbs less. Robust absorption of carbon requires a continuous cycling of colder, carbon-poor water upward from the ocean depths. If the global thermohaline conveyor [enormous volumes of cold, salty water are transported from the North Atlantic to the North Pacific, and warmer water is returned] were to fail, a dangerous drop in carbon absorption could result.

But the biggest threat to the oceanic carbon cycle lies in diminishing phytoplankton productivity. In the past 20 years, phytoplankton concentrations in northern oceans have decreased by as much as 30%. Scientists from NASA [National Aeronautics and Space Administration] and the National Oceanic and Atmospheric Administration suspect that warmer temperatures and low winds are depriving the phytoplankton of nitrogen and carbon dioxide. A Japanese researcher at Hokkaido University has noted a sharp drop in the amount of carbon dioxide absorbed by the northern Pacific Ocean over the past 15 years. Yutaka Watanabe has stated that the amount of carbon dioxide in the ocean has dropped by 10%.

The gravest concern is that rising temperatures on this planet will lead to a venting of methane from the oceans.

Melting Ice Feedback

Another feedback mechanism which is already beginning to work against us is the retreat of ice cover, particularly from the Arctic ice cap and from Greenland. The melting ice cover will trouble us in several ways. Freshwater runoff will help to disrupt thermohaline circulation in the oceans. . . . Melting ice cover would also raise ocean levels. . . . Satellite studies from NASA demonstrate that the Arctic ice cap is already retreating dramatically. A report released by the German Advisory Council on Global Change states that if the world's average temperature increases by more than 2°C beyond what it was at the beginning of the Industrial Revolution, it will likely trigger the melting of the Greenland ice cap and West Antarctic ice sheet. This would raise world sea levels by as much as 30 feet, submerging major cities such as New York, London, Tokyo, Miami, Bombay, Calcutta, Sydney, and Shanghai. The Hadley Centre for Climate Prediction and Research has stated that there are already sufficient greenhouse gases to raise Greenland's average temperature by 3°C by the middle of the century.

The retreating ice cover will decrease the Earth's albedo [solar energy reflected from the Earth back into space].... reflecting less of the sun's energy and resulting in a further warming of the Earth's surface. Evaporating melt waters could also increase the water vapor content in the lower atmosphere. Water vapor is a greenhouse gas. The result of both of these effects would be a positive feedback cycle where melting ice results in a warmer climate, which in turn leads to the melting of yet more ice.

And then there is the thawing tundra. Globally, frozen peatlands hold an estimated 550 billion tons of stored carbon. Dead plant matter is frozen in permafrost, slowing and even stopping the decomposition process. The slow, anaerobic decomposition which currently takes place in these frozen lands has produced a stockpile of methane which is already showing signs of escaping into the atmosphere as the tundra thaws. Methane has a shorter lifetime in the atmosphere than does carbon dioxide, but it is up to ten times as effective at trapping heat in the lower atmosphere. However, as the soils warm and the permafrost thaws, bacteria could set to work with a vengeance, decomposing plant matter at a higher rate, releasing carbon dioxide into the atmosphere instead of methane.

When Oceans Exhale

Each of these feedback mechanisms would have dire consequences for life on this planet. Taken together, they would reinforce each other and magnify the change in climate. But the gravest concern is that rising temperatures on this planet will lead to a venting of methane from the oceans. It is this possibility which is lamented in the above quotation from Stephen Hawking.

Methane is stored in the deep ocean along the continental margins, in the form of clathrates. These are massive deposits of carbonated slush, where the methane is trapped under pressure in the crystal lattices of frozen water (i.e., ice). Though the oceans hold much more methane than does the tundra, taken together they contain an estimated 2 trillion tons of methane in the form of clathrates.

The release of the entire balance of these pent up gases into the atmosphere is possible, but highly improbable. Dr. Hawking's scenario of an Earth superheated to match its sister planet, Venus, is unlikely. If the seas started venting methane into the atmosphere, the chances are that the process would halt before all of the sequestered methane escaped. However, just a portion of this enormous reserve of carbon, if released into the atmosphere, could render the planet uninhabitable. And while many scientists consider the possibility very remote, every day more investigators assess this scenario, shake their heads and wonder: could we already have set such an event into motion? . . .

Enter the End of the Hydrocarbon Era

The first reaction of most environmental activists to the news of peak oil is to say, "Good, we need to stop using fossil fuels anyway." It seems logical that a decline in hydrocarbon production will lead to a decline in carbon dioxide emissions. And it is likely that somewhere down the line, carbon emissions will abate simply due to the scarcity of fuel. But we will not go gently into that good night.

When you learn that heating costs are going to continue increasing and that shortages of natural gas are likely in our near future, what alternatives come to your mind for home heating? Passive solar heating? Sure, but that alone will not keep you warm on a cold winter night. Most people immediately think of wood. As heating costs go up, and as shortages put a chill on our homes, most of us are going to start burning wood. We will turn to biomass.

Burning biomass will likely add to our global warming problem, but it is probable that coal burning will be far more harmful.

Burning biomass is undoubtedly the dirtiest source of energy. As we burn wood, corn husks or cow chips to heat our homes, we will be pumping tremendous volumes of carbon into the atmosphere. And, in all probability, it is unavoidable. There are some things we can do to reduce the amount of wood we burn and so limit our contribution to global warming. Better insulation can increase efficiency. And consider the sort of wood furnace you will be using. Traditional brick fireplaces are the least efficient way to warm a house. Metal wood stoves are better, but soapstone is the best at holding heat and radiating it outward. A small load of wood in a soapstone stove can generate heat for hours. And when you are harvesting your wood, take care not to strip the forests bare. Be selective in choosing your wood. . . .

Burning biomass will likely add to our global warming problem, but it is probable that coal burning will be far more harmful. As oil and natural gas production go into decline in North America, the alternative we will ultimately turn to is coal—whether we like it or not. Coal is considered to be abundant in North America, and it is cheap. Despite all the talk of a hydrogen economy, the real investment will go into stepping up coal production. In fact, the production of coal-fired power plants has already been stepped up. As of February 2004, at least 100 new coal-fired electric power plants were planned to go up in more than 36 states. This new growth market is currently flying below [the] radar, because once plans for a coal-burning plant are made public, they are liable to be halted by the legislative efforts of environmentalists and neighborhood coalitions.

If even half of these plants are completed, they will increase exhaust gas emissions by 120 million cubic feet per minute. All the new coal plants being proposed would add one-tenth of one percent to the world's annual carbon dioxide emissions. That may not seem like much, but it is certainly a move in the wrong direction. And it is only the beginning.

As the production of oil and natural gas continues to slide, we will open up our coal reserves for electricity production, heating, industrial use, and to process coal into liquid transportation fuel. In the process, we will increase our exhaust emissions, rip up vast areas of land, create immense slag dumps, and pollute our waterways and groundwater. And we will require a major upgrade in our coal transportation network—that is, trucks and trains. You can expect strong efforts from industry and politicians to turn back environmental laws regulating coal production and coal burning. It will be argued that these regulations are damaging the economy. They will point to an economy choking from a constricting energy base, and they will insist that they cannot provide the energy we so desperately need with all these legal restrictions. Power outages will act to blunt the environmental sensibilities of the public.

Peak oil will not be a blessing in disguise with regard to global warming.

Perhaps the only salvation here lies in recent research that coal is likely to peak sometime around 2032, if not sooner. This will leave us a little less than 20 years of stepped up production before coal joins the list of has-beens. Then our carbon emissions really may begin to decrease.

But the US is not the only country likely to turn to coal. China is also eyeing its large reserves of coal, as is India. If the world's two most populous countries step up their coal consumption along with the US, then the decline in petroleum and natural gas production will actually be greeted with a pronounced increase in carbon emissions.

Peak oil will not be a blessing in disguise with regard to global warming. The models of global climate change developed by the IPCC [United Nations International Panel on Climate Change] and others have not taken into account the impacts of Peak Oil and the North American Natural Gas Cliff. These models are based on faulty economic projections produced by neo-classical economics—a warped discipline which is blind to resource depletion. If we turn to coal and biomass to make up for the decrease in oil and natural gas production, then it is likely that our actions will push the average global temperature well beyond the 6°C threshold mentioned above. The end of the oil age could very well push us into an age of runaway global warming.

Coal will not be able to support the kind of energy-intensive economy which we have built on oil and natural gas. It will be a faltering effort from a civilization in denial, intent on clinging to unsustainable ways. It will fail in the end, but in this last mad burn-off of energy resources, we may very well incur the demise of life on this planet.

CHAPTER 4

What Action Should Be Taken to Reduce Global Warming?

Chapter Preface

One key international response to global warming is the Kyoto Protocol, often called simply the Kyoto treaty. This agreement was negotiated in Kyoto, Japan, in December 1997 as an amendment to the United Nations Framework Convention on Climate Change (UNFCCC), an international treaty on global warming. Kyoto went into effect in 2005 and set mandatory targets for the reduction of greenhouse gases, understood to be the chief cause of rising global temperatures, for developed countries that had signed and ratified the treaty. Specifically, the Kyoto Protocol seeks to limit the global emissions of six greenhouse gases—carbon dioxide, methane, nitrous oxide, sulfur hexafluoride, haloalkanes (HFCs), and perfluorocarbons (PFCs)—by 5.2 percent as compared to 1990 emissions over a five-year period of 2008–2012. Under the terms of the treaty, each participating country is assigned a specific goal, with some countries facing much higher goals than others. As of the summer of 2007, 172 countries had ratified the Kyoto agreement.

The Kyoto Protocol attempts to achieve emissions reductions through two main strategies. One is a "cap-and-trade" system that allows participating countries (and in some cases states or regions within those countries) to trade emissions credits. Under this arrangement, a country that cannot meet its emissions goal is permitted to purchase or trade for credits from countries that are exceeding their goals. This system encourages global emissions cuts without regard to their origin. A second strategy used under Kyoto is the Clean Development Mechanism, in which countries having problems meeting their emissions goals can offset their excess emissions by financing emissions-reducing projects in developing countries. A similar program, the Joint Implementation, is available to encourage emissions-reducing projects in Eastern Europe and countries that used to be part of the former Soviet Union.

From the beginning, however, the Kyoto treaty faced many obstacles, and some critics called it a failure. The most damaging blow was that the United States—the single largest source of carbon emissions, responsible for about 25 percent of global greenhouse gases—refused to ratify the treaty. U.S. presidents Bill Clinton and his successor George W. Bush never submitted the treaty to the U.S. Senate for ratification because both objected to the treaty's failure to cover developing nations. Rapidly developing China, for example, is the world's second-largest emitter of greenhouse gases, but neither it nor other rapidly developing countries such as India are required to reduce any carbon emissions under the terms of the present agreement. U.S. policy makers argued that this defect in Kyoto would place U.S. companies at a disadvantage and harm the U.S. economy. Australia, also a major source of carbon emissions, rejected the treaty for similar reasons. Without the United States and Australia, Kyoto became a treaty that primarily targeted Canada, Japan, and the European Union.

The treaty was further weakened as many important signatory countries had trouble meeting the treaty emissions targets and largely abandoned their emissions goals. Canada's emissions, for example, instead of shrinking to its target of 6 percent, grew by 26 percent over 1990 levels, and Canadian prime minister Stephen Harper, as quoted in a January 30, 2007, *CBC News* story, called the Kyoto Protocol a "socialist scheme" designed to suck money out of rich countries. Japan, too, had a 6 percent goal but experienced an 8.1 percent increase. The European Union, meanwhile, was criticized for handing out too many "cap-and-trade" credits and thereby reducing the pressure for meaningful emissions reductions. At the same time, China's emissions grew considerably, and it remained unregulated even though it was anticipated to overtake the United States as the world's largest source of greenhouse emissions by 2009, ten years earlier than once predicted. Moreover, even if Kyoto goals were completely met by 2012, experts say this would reduce global temperatures only slightly, not enough to stop global warming or its harmful consequences.

Representatives from around the world have met several times to discuss the future of the Kyoto targets after 2012, but there is still much disagreement about how to proceed. Despite Kyoto's flaws, many think it is a step in the right direction and remains the only viable path to reducing the emissions that are generating global warming. This faction hopes that Kyoto will be extended and that countries will become more receptive to the idea of emissions trading and more willing to make significant emissions cuts. Others argue that the calls for deep emissions cuts are wildly unrealistic and that it might already be too late to stop major climate change. The authors of the viewpoints in this chapter debate the controversial issue of what actions should be taken to address global warming.

The United Nations Calls for Urgent International Action on Global Warming

Environment News Service

Environment News Service *is a daily wire news service that provides environmental news to news sources around the world.*

Top United Nations [UN] officials joined climate experts ... [on July 31, 2007] in urging decisive action on a global scale to combat the challenges posed by climate change. "We cannot continue with business as usual," Secretary-General Ban Ki-moon told a General Assembly meeting on the issue at UN Headquarters in New York. He cited the findings of the UN Intergovernmental Panel on Climate Change which confirmed earlier this year that global warming is directly linked to human activities. "I believe this is just the kind of global challenge that the UN is best suited to address," said Ban. "I am gratified by the universal recognition that the UN climate process is the appropriate forum for negotiating future global action."

"I am determined to minimize the UN system's own carbon footprint, and to make this a climate-neutral organization," the secretary-general said. "To that end, I have launched a Greening the UN initiative. I have invited all heads of agencies and other UN bodies to work with me on a comprehensive plan covering our worldwide premises and operations."

The Need for a Global Assessment

The two-day informal debate that opened ... [in July 2007] is the first devoted exclusively to climate change. Delegates are seeking to translate the growing scientific consensus on the problem into a broad political consensus for action following alarming UN reports earlier this year on its potentially devastating effects. Ban called for "new thinking" to tackle the challenge, since how it is addressed "will define us, our era, and ultimately, our global legacy." He is convening a high-level meeting on climate change when the new Assembly session starts in September. Ban highlighted the need for a comprehensive global agreement under the UN Framework Convention on Climate Change. The Kyoto Protocol, the international community's current framework for reducing greenhouse gas emissions, expires in 2012, and Ban said countries must agree on a successor pact to be ready for ratification by 2009 to allow countries to enact it into law before the Kyoto Protocol expires.

Rich countries should work towards a target of around 75 percent [emission] cuts.

President of the General Assembly Sheikha Haya Rashed Al Khalifa spoke of the "cruel irony" of the disproportionate effects of climate change on the countries least responsible for it. "Greater variations of rainfall, combined with rising sea levels, will lead to more extreme weather, particularly in parts of Asia, sub-Saharan Africa and Latin America," she said at the opening of today's meeting. "We therefore have a special responsibility to help those countries most affected to adapt to climate change." Such efforts "should not be at the cost of economic growth, but to achieve it," she said, noting that "a global consensus can only be secured if all countries can share in the benefits from action to address" climate change.

The General Assembly debate itself is carbon neutral. The carbon emissions from both UN Headquarters and from the air travel to bring experts to New York have been off-set by investment in a biomass fuel project in Kenya.

Drastic Emission Cuts Proposed

Expert panelist Sir Nicholas Stern of the London School of Economics said, "The cost of strong and timely action in addressing the global causes and impacts of climate change [are] far less than that of inaction or timid and delayed responses." Stern's 2006 climate change report, "The Stern Review," received international attention for its conclusion that addressing the climate change issue now is the best economic choice. Speaking at a press conference at UN Headquarters, Stern proposed a nine-point plan, including a 50 percent cut by 2050 in world greenhouse gas emissions, relative to 1990 emission levels. Rich countries should work towards a target of around 75 percent cuts, he said, as well as specific targets for 2020.

Drastic emission cuts now are necessary.

Stern said that the risks of climate change could be reduced, though not eliminated, by an expenditure of one percent of world gross domestic product per year. Strong world carbon markets should be developed and made much more simple and transparent, he said. In Stern's view, investment in technology and in the science of climate change should increase and deforestation should be addressed energetically. Because of climate change, development will cost tens of billions more per year than previously understood, he predicted. Yet adaptation and mitigation technologies must be developed and development assistance promises delivered.

Panelist Sunita Narain, director of the Indian Centre for Science and Environment, told the press conference that the climate change discourse is becoming "locked in the politics of the past" and "how to move ahead is the issue at hand." Narain said the Kyoto Protocol had been too little too late, and drastic emission cuts now are necessary. If emissions are not controlled with the speed required, there will be dramatic changes in climate and the poor will suffer its worst impacts, she said, adding that the unpredictability of rainfall levels is the consequence of climate change most harmful to women's ability to care for themselves and their families. She suggested that the South, which has not built its energy systems, could try to find a "leap-frog" technology to make a quick transition to a low carbon economy.

Private Sector Action

Jim Rogers, chairman and CEO of Duke Energy, said his company is the third largest consumer of coal, the fourth largest nuclear operator, and the third largest emitter of carbon dioxide in the United States. The climate change question needs leadership not only from all governments, but also from the private sector and nongovernmental organizations around the world, he said.

In the United States, legislation on climate change is expected to be in place by 2010, said Rogers, who emphasized that companies cannot wait for that to happen. Initiatives are being undertaken, in which energy companies such as General Electric, Dupont and some 400 other major firms have formed into coalitions to advise the government.

Duke Energy is retrofitting 29 energy supply units to address the realities of a carbon-constrained world. The investment environment must also be changed to reflect the reality of climate change, Rogers said, projecting greater investments in new technologies. He said one way to address the problem is with "productivity gains" in the use of electricity, whereby energy efficiency products and services are delivered to consumers.

The General Assembly informal debate seeks to build momentum towards the high-level meeting in September [2007] and the upcoming negotiations under the Climate Change Convention in December [2007] in Bali, Indonesia.

The United States Must Reduce Its Carbon Emissions by 80 Percent by 2050

Emily Robinson

Emily Robinson is the press secretary for the Union of Concerned Scientists, a nonprofit membership organization of scientists and citizens that uses scientific analysis, policy development, and citizen advocacy to seek practical environmental solutions.

The Union of Concerned Scientists (UCS) has been working on solutions [to global warming] for decades. UCS experts have identified a suite of technological and policy solutions that would enable the United States to dramatically reduce emissions of heat-trapping gases that cause climate change. Currently [in 2007] the United States, with less than 5 percent of the world's population, is responsible for about 25 percent of the world's global warming emissions. Scientists around the world have warned that a global average temperature increase of 2 degrees Celsius (3.6 degrees Fahrenheit) above pre-industrial age levels would be extremely dangerous. To prevent that amount of warming, the United States must reduce its emissions by at least 80 percent of 2000 levels by mid-century. To reach that target, the United States needs to encourage greater energy efficiency in every sector of the economy and:

- Put a mandatory, steadily declining cap on global warming emissions

- Build more efficient, less-polluting cars

- Promote renewable energy sources

- Protect U.S. forests and help developing countries curb tropical deforestation

Fortunately there are readily available solutions that not only would protect the planet, but create new domestic jobs, save Americans billions of dollars annually, strengthen our national security, and protect public health at the same time.

A 35 mpg average by 2018 and a 4 percent improvement annually thereafter would ... cut global warming pollution by 523 million metric tons in 2025.

So how do we get there? With a change in public policy. There are a number of bills in Congress right now that would move the country in the right direction, including ones that would institute a carbon "cap-and-trade" program limiting global warming emissions, others establishing a standard for the amount of electricity that comes from clean, renewable energy sources, and still others that require automakers to significantly boost vehicle fuel economy.

Build More Efficient, Less-Polluting Cars

Producing and burning fuel to power cars and trucks produces 25 percent of U.S. global warming pollution. Reducing emissions from vehicles will require more efficient cars, cleaner fuels, and improved access to public transit and other methods to reduce travel. Increasing fuel efficiency would help combat global warming, reduce our nation's dependence on oil, and save consumers billions of dollars at the pump. A UCS analysis found that a 35 mpg average by 2018 and a 4 percent improvement annually thereafter would save Americans $31 billion, reduce oil demand by 3.1 million barrels per day, and cut global warming pollution by 523 million metric tons in 2025. Existing technology can deliver this performance while preserving today's acceleration, size and safety.

Boosting fuel economy isn't the only way to improve vehicles. Coupled with more efficient cars, clean hydrogen, renewable electricity and biofuels could reduce global warming pollution from the transportation sector. For example, a vehicle running on a mixture of 15 percent gasoline and 85 percent cellulosic ethanol (E85) (ethanol made from grasses, wood chips and other organic material) would emit 75 percent less global warming pollution. In the near term, vehicles running on E85 made from corn emit 10 to 30 percent less global warming pollution than those running on pure gasoline, depending on how the corn is grown and harvested. . . .

Requiring utilities to supply a minimum percentage of their electricity from renewable sources would spur development of cleaner [energy] alternatives.

UCS automotive engineers recently put together a blueprint for a vehicle that combines these solutions (plus an improved air conditioning system) to cut global warming pollution by more than 40 percent, exceeding the global warming pollution standard for cars and trucks adopted by California and 10 other states. Automakers are currently fighting those standards in court. The off-the-shelf elements in the UCS minivan package, dubbed the Vanguard, would add about $300 to its price, but operational savings would result in more than $1,300 in lifetime consumer savings, with a payback in less than two years. All of the technologies in the Vanguard are in vehicles on the road today, but automakers have yet to combine them all in one single package. For more information, go to: www.ucsusa.org/clean_vehicles/vehicles_health/ucs-vanguard.html.

Promote Renewable Energy Sources

Seventy percent of our nation's electricity comes from burning coal, natural gas or oil; this accounts for 33 percent of

U.S. global warming pollution. Clean, renewable energy sources, such as wind, solar, geothermal and bioenergy (but not including hydroelectricity), currently account for only 2.5 percent of the nation's electricity mix. We need to move toward turning that mix on its head.

A federal "renewable electricity standard" requiring utilities to supply a minimum percentage of their electricity from renewable sources would spur development of cleaner alternatives and save Americans money. A 2004 UCS study, which is being updated, found that a federal standard requiring 20 percent renewable electricity by 2020 would cut global warming pollution by the equivalent of taking tens of million cars off the road, save consumers tens of billions in lower electricity and natural gas bills, and create several hundred thousand new jobs. For more, go to: www.ucsusa.org/clean_energy/renewable_energy_basics/renewing-americas-economy.html.

Protect Our Forests

The United States must do more to protect its forests, which reduce global warming by taking up carbon dioxide. The EPA [Environmental Protection Agency] estimates that in 2005 forests and other "sinks" took up enough carbon dioxide to offset more than 11 percent of the gross U.S. global warming emissions (for more, see: www.epa.gov/climatechange/emissions/downloads06/07ES.pdf). More can be done to increase the carbon storage of U.S. forests. For example, timber managers could double the stored carbon in the forests in the Pacific Northwest and Southeast if they lengthened the time between harvests and allowed older trees to remain standing.

We need an integrated set of policies, and Congress is beginning to take a hard look at some of them.

The United States also must do more to help developing countries protect and restore their forests. Tropical deforestation now accounts for about 20 percent of all human-caused carbon dioxide emissions each year. Many forest-rich developing countries are seeking to slow deforestation and help contribute to the effort to slow climate change. The United States should develop partnerships with developing countries to help them reduce emissions from tropical deforestation.

Policies to Get Us There

To significantly increase vehicle fuel economy, transition to renewable energy, ramp up energy efficiency, and protect forests at home and abroad, we need an integrated set of policies, and Congress is beginning to take a hard look at some of them.

Cap and trade: An economy wide cap-and-trade program would put a price on global warming pollution and harness the power of the market to cut emissions efficiently. Under such a program, a cap is set at a level of emissions based on scientific findings, and allowances are issued that correspond to a metric ton of global warming emissions. The allowances are distributed to emitters that are free to trade the permits, while reducing their overall emissions to match the cap level. Those facilities that can reduce emissions cheaply can sell their extra allowances to companies facing higher reduction costs. Emissions then would be cut in the most cost-effective manner.

A well-designed program would have a stringent cap on emissions designed to keep global average temperatures below a 2 degrees Celsius rise above pre-industrial age levels, cover all sources of emissions in the U.S. economy, and require all allowances to be auctioned rather than given away.

A cap-and-trade program will not be sufficient on its own. It should be implemented with policies that make it easier and more affordable to achieve limits on global warming pollution.

Two bills in Congress contain all of these elements. The Safe Climate Act in the House and the Global Warming Pollution Reduction Act in the Senate both establish a long-term framework to gradually reduce global warming emissions by at least 80 percent below 1990 levels by 2050, while providing flexibility to help companies meet the pollution reducton goals through a cap-and-trade program. The bills also call for a greater reliance on clean, renewable energy sources and improved energy efficiency—solutions that would have far-reaching positive results, such as cutting air pollution, protecting public health, creating new jobs, and reducing our dependence on oil.

Fuel efficiency and biofuels: Studies by the National Academy of Sciences, the Massachusetts Institute of Technology, the American Council for an Energy Efficient Economy, and UCS all show that existing technology can easily improve fuel economy by 4 percent per year (to 34 to 35 mpg over 10 years), the proposal President Bush set forth in his 2007 State of the Union address. Over the life of these more fuel efficient vehicles, savings at the pump would pay for the added technology in a few years, saving a net of $3,400, assuming gasoline costs $2.50 per gallon.

The president's proposal is almost identical to House and Senate bills that address fuel economy. Legislation introduced by Reps. Edward Markey (D-Mass.) and Todd Platts (R-Pa.) calls for new vehicle fleets to average 35 miles per gallon by 2018 and requires automakers to improve fuel economy by 4 percent annually thereafter (unless it is technologically infeasible). A similar bill in the Senate, known as "10-in-10," would require average vehicle fuel economy to attain 35 miles per gallon by 2019. And Sens. Byron Dorgan (D-N.D.) and Larry Craig (R-Idaho) have introduced a bill that also would raise fuel efficiency by 4 percent annually. For more information, go to: http://www.ucsusa.org/clean_vehicles/fuel_econ omy/10-in-10-CAFE-Bill.html.

In his 2007 State of the Union address, the president also proposed a goal to produce 35 billion gallons of renewable and alternative fuel by 2017. If this goal is met primarily with ethanol, UCS analysis shows that the initiative would reduce global warming pollution by 160 million metric tons in 2017, the equivalent of taking nearly 24 million of today's cars and trucks off the road. However, that would require construction of more than 40 ethanol production plants per year starting today. A better approach would be to adopt a national version of California's low carbon fuel standard, which would drive down global warming pollution from fuels by 10 percent in 2020 and add provisions to ensure low carbon fuels are produced sustainably. This would also ensure that the president's goal is not met by producing gasoline or diesel from coal, since liquid coal could increase global warming pollution by as much as 80 percent for every gallon used.

Renewable energy: A proposed House bill creating a national renewable electricity standard would require utilities to gradually increase renewable energy sources such as wind, solar, geothermal and bioenergy to 20 percent of total U.S. electricity use by 2020. Similar policies have already been enacted in 22 states and Washington, D.C. The Senate has passed a 10 percent by 2020 national renewable electricity standard three times since 2002—most recently in June 2005.

An Energy Revolution Is Needed to Create a Sustainable Energy System

Sven Teske, Arthouros Zervos, and Oliver Schaefer

Sven Teske, Arthouros Zervos, and Oliver Schaefer authored this report published by Greenpeace International and the European Renewable Energy Council. Greenpeace International is an independent global campaigning organization dedicated to protecting and conserving the environment and promoting peace. The European Renewable Energy Council is an umbrella organization of the European renewable energy industry, trade, and research associations active in the sectors of bioenergy, geothermal, ocean, small hydropower, solar electricity, solar thermal, and wind energy.

Global climate change caused by the relentless build-up of greenhouse gases in the earth's atmosphere is already disrupting ecosystems and is already causing about 150,000 additional deaths per year. An average global warming of 2°C threatens millions of people with an increased risk of hunger, malaria, flooding and water shortages. If rising temperatures are to be kept within acceptable limits then we need to significantly reduce our greenhouse gas emissions. This makes both environmental and economic sense. The main greenhouse gas is carbon dioxide (CO_2) produced by using fossil fuels for energy and transport.

Renewable Energy and Energy Efficiency

Spurred by recent large increases in the price of oil, the issue of security of supply is now at the top of the energy policy agenda. One reason for these price increases is the fact that

Sven Teske, Arthouros Zervos, and Oliver Schaefer, from *Energy [R]evolution: A Sustainable World Energy Outlook.* Amsterdam: The Netherlands, Greenpeace International and European Renewable Energy Council, 2007. www.greenpeace.org. Reproduced by permission.

supplies of all fossil fuels—oil, gas and coal—are becoming scarcer and more expensive to produce. The days of "cheap oil and gas" are coming to an end. Uranium, the fuel for nuclear power, is also a finite resource. By contrast, the reserves of renewable energy that are technically accessible globally are large enough to provide about six times more power than the world currently consumes—forever.

Renewable energy technologies vary widely in their technical and economic maturity, but there are a range of sources which offer increasingly attractive options. These sources include wind, biomass, photovoltaic, solar thermal, geothermal, ocean and hydroelectric power. Their common feature is that they produce little or no greenhouse gases, and rely on virtually inexhaustible natural sources for their "fuel". Some of these technologies are already competitive. Their economics will further improve as they develop technically, as the price of fossil fuels continues to rise and as their saving of carbon dioxide emissions is given a monetary value.

The climate change imperative demands nothing short of an energy revolution.

At the same time there is enormous potential for reducing our consumption of energy, while providing the same level of energy 'services'. This study details a series of energy efficiency measures which together can substantially reduce demand in industry, homes, business and services.

The solution to our future energy needs lies in greater use of renewable energy sources for both heat and power. Nuclear power is not the solution as it poses multiple threats to people and the environment. These include the risks and environmental damage from uranium mining, processing and transport, the risk of nuclear weapons proliferation, the unsolved problem of nuclear waste and the potential hazard of a serious accident. The nuclear option is therefore eliminated in this analysis.

The Energy Revolution

The climate change imperative demands nothing short of an energy revolution. At the core of this revolution will be a change in the way that energy is produced, distributed and consumed. The five key principles behind this shift will be to:

- Implement renewable solutions, especially through decentralised energy systems

- Respect the natural limits of the environment

- Phase out dirty, unsustainable energy sources

- Create greater equity in the use of resources

- Decouple economic growth from the consumption of fossil fuels Decentralised energy systems, where power and heat are produced close to the point of final use, avoid the current waste of energy during conversion and distribution. They will be central to the Energy [R]evolution, as will the need to provide electricity to the two billion people around the world to whom access is presently denied. . . .

The Energy [R]evolution Scenario has a target for the reduction of worldwide emissions by 50% below 1990 levels by 2050, with per capita carbon dioxide emissions reduced to less than 1.3 tonnes per year in order for the increase in global temperature to remain under +2°C. A second objective is to show that this is even possible with the global phasing out of nuclear energy. To achieve these targets, the scenario is characterised by significant efforts to fully exploit the large potential for energy efficiency. At the same time, cost-effective renewable energy sources are accessed for both heat and electricity generation, as well as the production of biofuels.

Today, renewable energy sources account for 13% of the world's primary energy demand. Biomass, which is mainly used for heating, is the largest renewable source. The share of renewable energy in electricity generation is 18%, whilst the contribution of renewables to heat supply is around 26%. About 80% of primary energy supply still comes from fossil fuels, and the remaining 7% from nuclear power.

A balanced and timely mobilisation of all renewable technologies is of great importance.

The Energy [R]evolution Scenario describes a development pathway which transforms the present situation into a sustainable energy supply.

- Exploitation of the large energy efficiency potential will reduce primary energy demand from the current 435,00 PJ/a (Peta Joules per year) to 422,000 PJ/a by 2050. Under the reference scenario there would be an increase to 810,000 PJ/a. This dramatic reduction is a crucial prerequisite for achieving a significant share of renewable energy sources, compensating for the phasing out of nuclear energy and reducing the consumption of fossil fuels.

- The increased use of combined heat and power generation (CHP) also improves the supply system's energy conversion efficiency, increasingly using natural gas and biomass. In the long term, decreasing demand for heat and the large potential for producing heat directly from renewable energy sources limits the further expansion of CHP.

- The electricity sector will be the pioneer of renewable energy utilisation. By 2050, around 70% of electricity will be produced from renewable energy sources, in cluding large hydro. An installed capacity of 7,100 GW will produce 21,400 Terawatt hours per year (TWh/a) of electricity in 2050.

- In the heat supply sector, the contribution of renewables will increase to 65% by 2050. Fossil fuels will be increasingly replaced by more efficient modern technologies, in particular biomass, solar collectors and geothermal.

- Before biofuels can play a substantial rule in the transport sector, the existing large efficiency potentials have to be exploited. In this study, biomass is primarily committed to stationary applications; the use of biofuels for transport is limited by the availability of sustainably grown biomass.

- By 2050, half of primary energy demand will be covered by renewable energy sources.

Following stringent environmental targets in the energy sector also pays off in economic terms.

To achieve an economically attractive growth of renewable energy sources a balanced and timely mobilisation of all renewable technologies is of great importance. This depends on technical potentials, actual costs, cost reduction potentials and technological maturity.

Decreasing Emissions and Costs

Whilst worldwide CO_2 emissions will almost double under the reference scenario by 2050—far removed from a sustainable development path—under the Energy [R]evolution Scenario emissions will decrease from 23,000 million tonnes in 2003 to 11,500 million tonnes in 2050. Annual per capita emissions will drop from 4.0 t to 1.3 t. In the long run, efficiency gains and the increased use of biofuels will even reduce CO_2 emissions in the transport sector. With a share of 36% of total CO_2 emissions in 2050, the power sector will be overtaken by the transport sector as the largest source of emissions.

Due to the growing demand for power, we are facing a significant increase in society's expenditure on electricity supply. Under the reference scenario, the undiminished growth in demand, the increase in fossil fuel prices and the costs of CO_2 emissions all result in electricity supply costs rising from today's [2007's] $1,130 billion per year to more than $4,300 bn per year in 2050. The Energy [R]evolution Scenario not only complies with global CO_2 reduction targets but also helps to stabilise energy costs and thus relieve the economic pressure on society. Increasing energy efficiency and shifting energy supply to renewable energy resources leads to long term costs for electricity supply that are one third lower than in the reference scenario. It becomes obvious that following stringent environmental targets in the energy sector also pays off in economic terms.

To make the energy [r]evolution real and avoid dangerous climate change, the following assumptions need to be implemented:

- The phasing out of all subsidies for fossil fuels and nuclear energy and the internalisation of external costs

- The setting out of legally binding targets for renewable energy

- The provision of defined and stable returns for investors

- Guaranteed priority access to the grid for renewable generators

- Strict efficiency standards for all energy consuming appliances, buildings and vehicles

Individuals Can Also Help Reduce Global Warming

Larry West

Larry West is a professional writer and editor who has written many articles about environmental issues for leading newspapers, magazines, and online publications.

Burning fossil fuels such as natural gas, coal, oil and gasoline raises the level of carbon dioxide in the atmosphere, and carbon dioxide is a major contributor to the greenhouse effect and global warming. You can help to reduce the demand for fossil fuels, which in turn reduces global warming, by using energy more wisely. Here are 10 simple actions you can take to help reduce global warming.

1. *Reduce, reuse, recycle.* Do your part to reduce waste by choosing reusable products instead of disposables. Buying products with minimal packaging (including the economy size when that makes sense for you) will help to reduce waste. And whenever you can, recycle paper, plastic, newspaper, glass and aluminum cans. If there isn't a recycling program at your workplace, school or in your community, ask about starting one. By recycling half of your household waste, you can save 2,400 pounds of carbon dioxide annually.

2. *Use less heat and air conditioning.* Adding insulation to your walls and attic, and installing weather stripping or caulking around doors and windows can lower your heating costs more than 25 percent, by reducing the amount of energy you need to heat and cool your home. Turn down the heat while you're sleeping at night

Larry West, "Top 10 Things You Can Do to Reduce Global Warming," *About.com*, 2007. http://environment.about.com. Copyright © 2006 About, Inc., a part of The New York Times Company. All rights reserved. Reproduced by permission.

or away during the day, and keep temperatures moderate at all times. Setting your thermostat just 2 degrees lower in winter and higher in summer could save about 2,000 pounds of carbon dioxide each year.

3. *Change a light bulb.* Wherever practical, replace regular light bulbs with compact fluorescent light (CFL) bulbs. Replacing just one 60-watt incandescent light bulb with a CFL will save you $30 over the life of the bulb. CFLs also last 10 times longer than incandescent bulbs, use two-thirds less energy, and give off 70 percent less heat. If every U.S. family replaced one regular light bulb with a CFL, it would eliminate 90 billion pounds of greenhouse gases, the same as taking 7.5 million cars off the road.

4. *Drive less and drive smart.* Less driving means fewer emissions. Besides saving gasoline, walking and biking are great forms of exercise. Explore your community's mass transit system, and check out options for carpooling to work or school. When you do drive, make sure your car is running efficiently. For example, keeping your tires properly inflated can improve your gas mileage by more than 3 percent. Every gallon of gas you save not only helps your budget, it also keeps 20 pounds of carbon dioxide out of the atmosphere.

5. *Buy energy-efficient products.* When it's time to buy a new car, choose one that offers good gas mileage. Home appliances now come in a range of energy-efficient models, and compact fluorescent bulbs are designed to provide more natural-looking light while using far less energy than standard light bulbs. Avoid products that come with excess packaging, especially molded plastic and other packaging that can't be recycled. If you reduce your household garbage by 10 percent, you can save 1,200 pounds of carbon dioxide annually.

6. *Use less hot water.* Set your water heater at 120-degrees to save energy, and wrap it in an insulating blanket if it is more than 5 years old. Buy low-flow showerheads to save hot water and about 350 pounds of carbon dioxide yearly. Wash your clothes in warm or cold water to reduce your use of hot water and the energy required to produce it. That change alone can save at least 500 pounds of carbon dioxide annually in most households. Use the energy-saving settings on your dishwasher and let the dishes air-dry.

7. *Use the "off" switch.* Save electricity and reduce global warming by turning off lights when you leave a room, and using only as much light as you need. And remember to turn off your television, video player, stereo and computer when you're not using them. It's also a good idea to turn off the water when you're not using it. While brushing your teeth, shampooing the dog or washing your car, turn off the water until you actually need it for rinsing. You'll reduce your water bill and help to conserve a vital resource.

8. *Plant a tree.* If you have the means to plant a tree, start digging. During photosynthesis, trees and other plants absorb carbon dioxide and give off oxygen. They are an integral part of the natural atmospheric exchange cycle here on Earth, but there are too few of them to fully counter the increases in carbon dioxide caused by automobile traffic, manufacturing and other human activities. A single tree will absorb approximately one ton of carbon dioxide during its lifetime.

9. *Get a report card from your utility company.* Many utility companies provide free home energy audits to help consumers identify areas in their homes that may not be energy efficient. In addition, many utility companies offer rebate programs to help pay for the cost of energy-efficient upgrades.

10. *Encourage others to conserve.* Share information about recycling and energy conservation with your friends, neighbors and co-workers, and take opportunities to encourage public officials to establish programs and policies that are good for the environment.

These 10 steps will take you a long way toward reducing your energy use and your monthly budget. And less energy use means less dependence on the fossil fuels that create greenhouse gases and contribute to global warming.

New Technologies Are the Only Solution to Global Warming

Robert J. Samuelson

Robert J. Samuelson is a columnist for the Washington Post, *a daily national newspaper published in Washington, D.C.*

> "Global warming may or may not be the great environmental crisis of the next century, but—regardless of whether it is or isn't—we won't do much about it. We will (I am sure) argue ferociously over it and may even, as a nation, make some fairly solemn-sounding commitments to avoid it. But the more dramatic and meaningful these commitments seem, the less likely they are to be observed. Little will be done. . . . Global warming promises to become a gushing source of national hypocrisy."—This column, July 1997

Well, so it has. In three decades of columns, I've never quoted myself at length, but here it's necessary. [Former Vice President] Al Gore calls global warming an "inconvenient truth," as if merely recognizing it could put us on a path to a solution. That's an illusion. The real truth is that we don't know enough to relieve global warming, and—barring major technological breakthroughs—we can't do much about it. This was obvious nine years ago; it's still obvious. Let me explain.

Difficult Choices

From 2003 to 2050, the world's population is projected to grow from 6.4 billion people to 9.1 billion, a 42 percent increase. If energy use per person and technology remain the same, total energy use and greenhouse gas emissions (mainly, carbon dioxide) will be 42 percent higher in 2050. But that's too low, because societies that grow richer use more energy. Unless we condemn the world's poor to their present poverty—and freeze everyone else's living standards—we need economic growth. With modest growth, energy use and greenhouse emissions [will] more than double by 2050.

Just keeping annual greenhouse gas emissions constant means that the world must somehow offset these huge increases. There are two ways: Improve energy efficiency, or shift to energy sources with lower (or no) greenhouse emissions. Intuitively, you sense this is tough. China, for example, builds about one coal-fired power plant a week. Now a new report from the International Energy Agency [IEA] in Paris shows all the difficulties.

The IEA report assumes that existing technologies are rapidly improved and deployed. Vehicle fuel efficiency increases by 40 percent. In electricity generation, the share for coal (the fuel with the most greenhouse gases) shrinks from about 40 percent to about 25 percent—and much carbon dioxide is captured before going into the atmosphere. Little is captured today. Nuclear energy increases. So do "renewables" (wind, solar, biomass, geothermal); their share of global electricity output rises from 2 percent now to about 15 percent.

We're now powerless. We can't end annual greenhouse emissions, and once in the atmosphere, the gases seem to linger for decades.

Some of these changes seem heroic. They would require tough government regulation, continued technological gains and public acceptance of *higher* fuel prices. Never mind. Having postulated a crash energy diet, the IEA simulates five scenarios with differing rates of technological change. In each, greenhouse emissions in 2050 are higher than today. The increases vary from 6 percent to 27 percent.

Since 1800 there's been modest global warming. I'm unqualified to judge between those scientists (the majority) who blame man-made greenhouse gases and those (a small minority) who finger natural variations in the global weather system. But if the majority are correct, the IEA report indicates we're now powerless. We can't end annual greenhouse emissions, and once in the atmosphere, the gases seem to linger for decades. So concentration levels rise. They're the villains; they presumably trap the world's heat. They're already about 36 percent higher than in 1800. Even with its program, the IEA says another 45 percent rise may be unavoidable. How much warming this might create is uncertain; so are the consequences.

New Technology the Only Solution

I draw two conclusions—one political, one practical. No government will adopt the draconian restrictions on economic growth and personal freedom (limits on electricity usage, driving and travel) that might curb global warming. Still, politicians want to show they're "doing something." The result is grandstanding. Consider the Kyoto Protocol. It allowed countries that joined to castigate those that didn't. But it hasn't reduced carbon dioxide emissions (up about 25 percent since 1990), and many signatories didn't adopt tough enough policies to hit their 2008–2012 targets. By some estimates, Europe may overshoot by 15 percent and Japan by 25 percent.

The trouble with the global warming debate is that is has become a moral crusade when it's really an engineering problem.

Ambitious U.S. politicians also practice this self-serving hypocrisy. Gov. Arnold Schwarzenegger has a global warming program. Gore counts 221 cities that have "ratified" Kyoto. Some pledge to curb their greenhouse emissions. None of these programs will reduce global warming. They're public relations exercises and—if they impose costs—are undesirable. The practical conclusion is that if global warming is a potential calamity, the only salvation is new technology. I once received an e-mail from an engineer. Thorium, he said. I had never heard of thorium. It is, he argued, a nuclear fuel that is more plentiful and safer than uranium without waste disposal problems. It's an exit from the global warming trap. After reading many articles, I gave up trying to decide whether he is correct. But his larger point is correct: Only an aggressive research and development program might find ways of breaking our dependence on fossil fuels or dealing with it. Perhaps some system could purge the atmosphere of surplus greenhouse gases?

The trouble with the global warming debate is that it has become a moral crusade when it's really an engineering problem. The inconvenient truth is that if we don't solve the engineering problem, we're helpless.

Humans Must Learn to Adapt to Global Warming

Roger Pielke Jr.

Roger Pielke Jr. is director of the Center for Science and Technology Policy Research at the University of Colorado.

It is good news that debate over climate change is moving from arguments over the science to arguments over policy. But don't expect the policy arguments to be any less intense. One important point of contention is the proper role of adaptation to climate impacts in climate policy, which to date has received far too little attention as compared to the attention paid to energy policies, called climate mitigation.

Adaptation Is More Effective than Mitigation

The first thing to recognize about climate policy is that any successful efforts to reduce carbon dioxide emissions today [October 2006] will not have a perceptible impact on the climate for many decades. This of course does not mean that we need not concern ourselves with reducing emissions. To the contrary, it means that to succeed politically and economically we have to develop creative strategies that connect shorter terms benefits of emissions reductions with those benefits expected in the more distant future.

But what should be unavoidably obvious about the delay between any reduction in emissions and their corresponding effects on climate is that the only policies that can have a perceptible effect on the impacts of climate are necessarily adaptive in nature.

Consider the case of hurricanes. While research continues into the exact role of human-caused climate change in recent hurricane activity, let's simply assume that greenhouse gas emissions have led to an increase in hurricane intensities and will continue to do so into the future. What effect would mitigation of greenhouse gases have on future global economic losses? Depending on various assumptions for growth in population and the economy, exact changes in hurricane intensity, and the relation between intensity and damage it turns out that adaptation in the form of, for example, improved building codes and construction, is between 10 and 25 times more effective than would be the effects of a fully-successful Kyoto Protocol. And under every emissions reduction scenario, even a magic instant curtailment of global emissions, adaptation is by far the more effective approach to future hurricane damage across assumptions.

Does this mean that the Kyoto Protocol is in general a bad idea? Of course not. What it does mean however is that with respect to future hurricane impacts, adaptation should be the focal point of discussions related to climate policy. The reality is that hurricanes are discussed far more in terms of justifications for changes in energy policies, which is misleading at best. Similar results have been found for the important role of adaptation with respect to future impacts of floods, tornadoes, and other extreme events.

Protecting People Today and Future Generations

Given knowledge of the significant benefits of adaptive responses one of the great puzzles of the debate over climate change is how people who express great concern about the plight of future generations expected to experience the impacts of changes in climate can be simultaneously apparently so callus about those who suffer climate impacts in today's generation. Images of poor people suffering in the aftermath of Hurricane Katrina are more often used to justify changes in energy policies than to recommend those adaptive actions that might have an appreciable impact on the lives of those who suffer the effects of today's disasters.

Some blame for this situation must be placed at the feet of the international response to climate change. The Climate Convention has defined climate change in such a way that creates a bias against adaptation. In practice this means that it has been extremely difficult for countries with profound vulnerabilities to receive funding to increase their resilience. By contrast, it is far easier to obtain funding for mitigation actions focused on energy policies. The structure of the international response has also motivated advocacy efforts in support of its agenda biased against adaptation.

Given the wide base of research and experience that supports the effectiveness of adaptive policies, advocates of action on climate change should be careful. To the extent that they ignore adaptation in their advocacy efforts, they risk advancing poor policy arguments for needed responses to climate change. This would be a shame because climate change, and a human role in it, is worthy of our concern. Even if it is inconvenient for some agendas, all policy options should be on the table, especially adaptation.

Organizations to Contact

The editors have compiled the following list of organizations concerned with the issues debated in this book. The descriptions are derived from materials provided by the organizations. All have publications or information available for interested readers. The list was compiled on the date of publication of the present volume; the information provided here may change. Readers need to remember that many organizations take several weeks or longer to respond to inquiries.

Climate Solutions
219 Legion Way SW, Suite 201, Olympia, WA   98501-1113
(360) 352-1763 • fax: (360) 943-4977
e-mail: info@climatesolutions.org
Web site: www.climatesolutions.org

Climate Solutions is a nonprofit organization located in the Pacific Northwest, formed in 1998 to develop ways to act decisively and creatively toward addressing the global warming crisis. The group's Web site contains background information on global warming, discusses solutions, and provides a variety of publications on the subject.

Global Warming International Center
PO Box 50303, Palo Alto, CA
(630) 910-1551 • fax: (630) 910-1561
Web site: www.globalwarming.net

The Global Warming International Center is an international body that disseminates information on global warming science and policy and sponsors research to help the understanding and mitigation of global warming. News releases, press statements, and a variety of papers on global warming can be found on the group's Web site.

Hudson Institute
1015 Fifteenth St. NW, Floor 6, Washington, DC   20005
(202) 974-2400 • fax: (202) 974-2410
e-mail: info@hudson.org
Web site: www.hudson.org

The Hudson Institute is a nonpartisan policy research organization dedicated to research and analysis aimed at promoting global security, prosperity, and freedom. A search of the group's Web site produces a list of articles and commentaries on issues relating to global warming, many of them critical of mainstream advocacy on this issue.

National Resources Defense Council (NRDC)
40 W. Twentieth St., New York, NY   10011
(212) 727-2700 • fax: (212) 727-1773
e-mail: nrdcinfo@nrdc.org
Web site: www.nrdc.org/globalWarming

The National Resources Defense Council is an environmental organization that uses law, science, and the support of 1.2 million members and online activists to protect the planet's wildlife and wild places and to ensure a safe and healthy environment for all living things. The NRDC Web site contains a special section on global warming that provides many articles and reports on the issue.

Pew Center on Global Climate Change
2101 Wilson Blvd., Suite 550, Arlington, VA   22201
(703) 516-4146 • fax: (703) 841-1422
Web site: www.pewclimate.org

The Pew Center on Global Climate Change is a nonprofit, independent organization founded to provide credible information and solutions on climate change. The center brings together business leaders, policy makers, scientists, and other experts to formulate a new approach to a complex and often controversial issue. The group's excellent Web site provides both basic and in-depth information and fact sheets on global warming, as well as access to Pew Center reports and links to a variety of other relevant materials.

Reason Foundation
3415 S. Sepulveda Blvd., Suite 400
Los Angeles, CA   90034-6064
(310) 391-2245 • fax: (310) 391-4395
Web site: www.reason.org

The Reason Foundation is a national public policy research organization that promotes libertarian principles, including individual liberty, free markets, and the rule of law. The foundation publishes the monthly magazine, *Reason*, and a search of its Web site for global warming produces a long list of articles and commentaries on this topic.

Union of Concerned Scientists (UCS)
2 Brattle Square, Cambridge, MA   02238-9105
(617) 547-5552 • fax: (617) 864-9405
Web site: www.ucsusa.org

The Union of Concerned Scientists is a science-based non-profit organization that works to create a healthy environment and a safer world. Using independent scientific research and citizen action, UCS proposes solutions to environmental problems and works to secure necessary changes in government policy, corporate practices, and consumer choices. The UCS Web site contains a highly informative section on global warming, including information on the science behind the phenomenon and possible solutions.

United Nations Convention on Climate Change (UNFCCC)
PO Box 260124, Bonn   D-53153
  Germany
(49-228) 815-1000 • fax: (49-228) 815-1999
e-mail: secretariat@unfccc.int
Web: http://unfccc.int

The United Nations Convention on Climate Change (UNFCCC) is the first international treaty on climate change. This United Nations Web site offers information about this and a subsequent treaty, the Kyoto Protocol, including a *UN-FCCU E-Newsletter*, which provides an overview of major news and announcements on global warming issues.

United Nations Intergovernmental Panel on Climate Change (UNIPCC)

IPCC Secretariat, C/O World Meteorological Organization, 7bis Ave. de la Paix, C.P. 2300, Geneva 2 CH-1211 Switzerland
+41-22-730-8208 • fax: +41-22-730-8025
e-mail: IPCC-Sec@wmo.int
Web site: www.ipcc-wg2.org

The Intergovernmental Panel on Climate Change (IPCC) was established by the United Nations Environmental Programme (UNEP) and the World Meteorological Organization (WMO) in 1988 to assess the scientific, technical, and socioeconomic information relating to human-induced climate change, its potential impacts, and possible solutions. The IPCC Web site is a source for IPCC assessment reports, technical papers, and other publications.

U.S. Global Change Research Program

1717 Pennsylvania Ave. NW, Suite 250
Washington, DC 20006
(202) 223-6262 • fax: (202) 223-3065
e-mail: information@usgcrp.gov
Web site: www.usgcrp.gov

The U.S. Global Change Research Program was established by the president in 1989 and was continued by Congress in the Global Change Research Act of 1990. The program supports research on the issue of natural and human-induced climate changes and the implications of climate change for society. The Web site contains information about the effects of global warming on the United States as well as other articles and materials.

World Wildlife Fund (WWF)
1250 Twenty-Fourth St. NW, Washington, DC   20090-7180
(202) 293-4800 • fax: (202) 293-9211
Web site: www.panda.org/about_wwf/what_we_do/climate_
change/index.cfm

The World Wildlife Fund (WWF) is one of the largest conservation organizations, with almost 5 million supporters in more than one hundred countries. WWF's mission is to stop the degradation of the planet's natural environment and to build a future in which humans live in harmony with nature. The WWF Web site contains a helpful section on climate change that provides much information about the global warming problem, its impact, and possible solutions.

Bibliography

Books

D. P. Agin	*Junk Science: How Politicians, Corporations, and Other Hucksters Betray Us*, New York: Thomas Dunne Books, 2006.
Lester Russell Brown	*Outgrowing the Earth: The Food Security Challenge in the Age of Falling Water Tables and Rising Temperatures*, New York: Norton, 2004.
Tim F. Flannery	*The Weather Makers: How Man Is Changing the Climate and What It Means for Life on Earth*, New York: Atlantic Monthly Press, 2005.
Ross Gelbspan	*Boiling Point: How Politicians, Big Oil and Coal, Journalists, and Activists Are Fueling the Climate Crisis—and What We Can Do to Avert Disaster*, New York: Basic Books, 2004.
Al Gore	*An Inconvenient Truth: The Crisis of Global Warming*, New York: Viking, 2007.
Christopher C. Homer	*The Politically Incorrect Guide to Global Warming and Environmentalism*, Washington, DC: Regnery, 2007.
Elizabeth Kolbert	*Field Notes from a Catastrophe: Man, Nature, and Climate Change*, London: Bloomsbury, 2006.

J. E. Lovelock — *The Revenge of Gaia: Earth's Climate in Crisis and the Fate of Humanity*, New York: Basic Books, 2006.

Chris Mooney — *Storm World: Hurricanes, Politics, and the Battle Over Global Warming*, Orlando, FL: Harcourt, 2007.

Anne F. Rockwell — *Why Are the Ice Caps Melting? The Dangers of Global Warming*, New York: Collins, 2006.

S. Fred Singer — *Unstoppable Global Warming: Every 1,500 Years*, Lanham, MD: Rowman & Littlefield, 2007.

David Steinman — *Safe Trip to Eden: 10 Steps to Save Planet Earth from the Global Warming Meltdown*, New York: Thunder's Mouth Press, 2007.

Henrik Svensmark — *The Chilling Stars: A New Theory of Climate Change*, London: Icon, 2007.

William Sweet — *Kicking the Carbon Habit: Global Warming and the Case for Renewable and Nuclear Energy*, New York: Columbia University Press, 2006.

Michael Tennesen — *The Complete Idiot's Guide to Global Warming*, New York: Alpha Books, 2004.

Peter Douglas Ward — *Under a Green Sky: Global Warming, the Mass Extinctions of the Past, and What They Mean for Our Future*, New York: Smithsonian Books/ Collins, 2007.

Spencer R. Weart   *The Discovery of Global Warming,*
                    Boston: Harvard University Press,
                    2003.

Periodicals

Ronald Bailey   "Two Sides to Global Warming: Is It
                    Proven Fact, or Just Conventional
                    Wisdom?" *Reason Magazine,* Novem-
                    ber 10, 2004. www.reason.com/news/
                    show/34939.html.

Jules Boykoff and   "Journalistic Balance as Global
Maxwell Boykoff   Warming Bias: Creating Controversy
                    Where Science Finds Consensus,"
                    *Fairness & Accuracy In Reporting
                    (FAIR),* November–December 2004.
                    www.fair.org/index.php?page=1978.

Canadian Wildlife "Climate Change and Wildlife," De-
                    cember 2005, Vol. 11, Iss. 4, p. 5.

John Carey   "Global Warming; Consensus Is
                    Growing Among Scientists, Govern-
                    ments, and Business That They Must
                    Act Fast to Combat Climate Change,"
                    Business Week, August 16, 2004.

Gregg   "Global Warming: Who Loses—and
Easterbrook   Who Wins?" *Atlantic Monthly,* April
                    2007.

Economist (US)   "Drawing Lines in Melting Ice: The
                    Arctic," August 18, 2007.

Energy Resource   "Survey: Vast Majority of Americans
                    Concerned about Climate Change,"
                    August 22, 2007.

Fire	"Climate Change Stretches Fire Crews," October 2006.
Global Agenda	"Clean Green Flying Machine? Planes Are Becoming Less Dirty, But There Are More of Them: Will It Ever Be Green to Fly?" August 15, 2007.
Mark Hertsgaard	"Killer Weather Ahead," *Nation*, February 26, 2007.
Elizabeth Kolbert	"The Climate of Man: III," *New Yorker*, May 9, 2005.
Jon Meacham	"The Editor's Desk: Facebook's Mark Zuckerberg: ExxonMobil on Global Warming," *Newsweek*, August 20, 2007.
Newsweek	"Greenhouse Simplicities," August 20, 2007.
Petroleum Economist	"Alternative Realities," March 2007.
Dale Allen Pfeiffer	"Global Climate Change and Peak Oil," *Wilderness Publications*, 2004. www.fromthewilderness.com/free/ww3/041304_climate_change_pt1.html.
Philip Pullella	"Global Warming Will Increase World Hunger: UN," *Reuters News Service*, May 27, 2005.

Mark Scott and Cassidy Flanagan
"Europe: No. 1 in Sustainable Energy; The EC is Committed to Policies that Include Subsidies for Alternative Energy and Encourage Investment in New Technologies," *Business Week Online*, August 6, 2007.

Stephanie Sims
"Go Green or No Home: Green Building Is Gaining Popularity and Rick Hunter, Managing Partner of Sage Homebuilders, Says His Company Is Capitalizing on It While Helping to Improve the Environment," *Construction Today*, August 2007.

Space Daily
"Climate Change Goes Underground," August 24, 2007.

Space Daily
"The Human Contribution to Atmosphere Circulation Changes," May 4, 2006.

Mark Shwartz
"Effects of Global Warming Already Being Felt on Plants and Animals Worldwide," January 3, 2003. http://news-service.stanford.edu/pr/03/root18.html.

Paul Sisco
"Are Global Warming Solutions Possible?" *Voice of America News*, August 15, 2006. www.voanews.com/english/archive/2006-08/2006-08-15-voa67.cfm.

James M. Taylor	"Discovery Refutes Alarmist Warming Claims," *Heartland Perspectives*, July 27, 2007. www.globalwarmingheartland.org/ article.cfm?artId=21732.
Mark Townsend and Paul Harris	"Now the Pentagon Tells Bush: Climate Change Will Destroy Us," *Observer*, February 22, 2004. http:// observer.guardian.co.uk/international/ story/0,6903,1153513,00.html.
Wayne Winegarden	"Fighting Global Warming the Liberal Way," *Townhall*, July 21, 2007. www.townhall.com/columnists/ WayneWinegarden/2007/07/21/ fighting_global_warming_the_liberal _way?page=full&comments=true.
Jennifer Winger	"An 'Unequivocal' Change: Monumental Report Leaves Little Doubt that Humans Have Hand in Climate Change," *Nature Conservancy*, summer 2007.
Fareed Zakaria	"Global Warming: Get Used to It," *Bulletin with Newsweek*, February 20, 2007.
Ernesto Zedillo	"Climate Change: Prudence or Venture?" *Forbes*, November 14.

Index